T0303036

Panpsychism

The Philosophy of the
Sensuous Cosmos

Panpsychism

The Philosophy of the
Sensuous Cosmos

Peter Ells

BOOKS

Winchester, UK
Washington, USA

First published by O-Books, 2011
O-Books is an imprint of John Hunt Publishing Ltd., Laurel House, Station Approach,
Alresford, Hants, SO24 9JH, UK
office1@o-books.net
www.o-books.com

For distributor details and how to order please visit the 'Ordering' section on our website.

Text copyright: Peter Ells 2010

ISBN: 978 1 84694 505 2

All rights reserved. Except for brief quotations in critical articles or reviews, no part of
this book may be reproduced in any manner without prior written permission from
the publishers.

The rights of Peter Ells as author have been asserted in accordance with the Copyright, Designs
and Patents Act 1988.

A CIP catalogue record for this book is available from the British Library.

Design: Stuart Davies

Printed in the UK by CPI Antony Rowe
Printed in the USA by Offset Paperback Mfrs, Inc

We operate a distinctive and ethical publishing philosophy in all
areas of our business, from our global network of authors to
production and worldwide distribution.

CONTENTS

For Elena
And for Ana María (1943-2003)

El amor viene en silencio,
Pero tú sabes cuando llega,
Pues ya nunca estarás solo,
Y no habrá tristeza en ti.

Acknowledgments

I would like to thank Herminio Martins who greatly encouraged me in writing this book. Thanks are also due to my supervisors at the University of Reading during the period I was taking my MA in Philosophy. Although they frequently disagreed with me profoundly, their discussion of my essays and dissertation helped to sharpen and improve the ideas expressed here. I also appreciate the editorial and production staff at O-Books for their skills and support of new authors and unorthodox ideas.

I would especially like to express my gratitude to Simon Weston OBE and his agents for their permission to quote from his book *Walking Tall* in my Chapter 9, *Pain and Suffering*.

Material World

Love comes in silence,
But you know when it has arrived,
Thereafter you will never be alone,
And never have sadness within you.

> Wedding card greeting, translated from Spanish

Why have I been sitting here at this computer keyboard, staring at the screen for the past hour, not knowing how to begin? I'm doing this, in part, because I want to be a writer. I want to become someone who shares my thoughts and feelings with others. Hhhhhhhhhhhh

I got stuck, and, waiting for inspiration to strike, I accidentally pressed the 'h' key, and my computer software helpfully capitalized the initial h.

Another 20 minutes have passed. Never mind. Let me tell you a little about myself. For 21 years I was married to Ana María. On the first of January 2003, four months ago as I write these words, she died after a long illness, and now her ashes lie in Wolvercote cemetery. Over the past several years, I have been trying to work out some meaning to my life, and it isn't easy. The harder I look, the harder it gets. This is especially so because I'm trying to be true both to:

- My personal experience as a human being
- Humankind's current scientific understanding.

My experience of the universe is that it is astonishingly and overwhelmingly beautiful. In 1995, Ana María and I, both of us secular, were invited to our first Quaker meeting by two gay friends of ours, Steve and Jon, who were getting married. It was a wonderful service, but I want to tell you about the meeting we attended two weeks later. Quaker meetings are based on silent worship, and I spent an hour, sitting in silence, looking at the vase of flowers resting on the central table.

Shortly before this, I had just finished reading *Consciousness Explained*, by Daniel Dennett (1991). His thesis is that consciousness, when understood as comprising qualitative, personal human experiences, does not exist. The word "consciousness" does have a meaning, Dennett says, but this is no more than a description of certain behavioral abilities that human beings have, such as the ability to talk about objects: "What a cute blue vase!" If, however, we actually believe that there is such a thing as an experience of blue, which corresponds to this utterance, then we are deluded. He mocks such a belief as nonsensical, likening it to a belief in "figment" in the brain, corresponding to pigment on the surface of the vase, (see his Chapter 12).

Sitting in the meeting, something happened that profoundly influenced me. The little voice in my head – the "me" that chatted, commented upon, analyzed and evaluated everything that I saw during the course of my waking life – stopped. For the first time in at least forty years I simply *experienced* the visual world. The peace and beauty of the room, the people, and the garden I could see through the window, all overwhelmed me with the force of a tidal wave...

"Wow! That was... "

And, with the beginning of that thought, the purity of this experience was at an end. Nonetheless, I was permanently changed. No longer could I think of the voice in my head as being "me". It was merely a portion of me, and my experiences were an equally important part of who I was as a person, and they did not need the validation of my internal commentary to establish their existence. Dennett, I was convinced, must be wrong.

Nonetheless I was utterly baffled because I did not have the least scintilla of an idea as to how consciousness might possibly be explained. From that time on, I developed an intense interest in the philosophy of consciousness, with a particular concern to understand how it must somehow fit into the natural, scientific order of the world. During the 1990's, there was an explosion of books on the subject. The anthology *The Nature of Consciousness – Philosophical Debates,* edited by Ned Block, Owen Flanagan and Güven Güzeldere (1997) was extremely useful. It contains a selection of seminal academic papers, such as *What Mary didn't know,* by Frank Jackson, and *What is it like to be a bat?* by Thomas Nagel, together with responses from their critics. Such collections are the best way to get into the topic because they provide a variety of opposing viewpoints. Most unusually, academic papers in this field are accessible to anyone who is prepared to study. Moreover, this particular collection was enhanced by having a thorough introductory overview by Güven Güzeldere.

By the summer of 2002, we both knew that Ana María was dying. We had to constrain our activities in accordance with her limitations, and I had to plan for my future without her. One activity we could still share was cooking, and this gave us great pleasure right to the end. That December, for example, we managed to have a traditional Christmas dinner with all the trimmings. Ana María contributed as much as she was able by peeling the vegetables. She wanted to do more, but I wouldn't let her get up from the table, because I was afraid that she would collapse.

As for myself, I was developing my thinking about consciousness, and fortunately I could do most of this work without leaving the house. In September 2002, I submitted an abstract for a short talk at the *Quantum Mind 2003* symposium, hosted by the University of Tucson, Arizona. To the delight of both of us, this was accepted. It meant, however, that I had to make some difficult choices. Much of my spare time I would spend keeping Ana María company, but I also spent a lot of my time alone in my room, working on my presentation. In March, after Ana María's funeral, I went to the symposium, and gave my talk. The friendly people there approached consciousness from an astonishing variety of viewpoints, and every day was crammed with inspiring and sometimes difficult lectures. The second leg of my trip was to Florida, to visit our niece and nephew, Rosana and Luis.

Personhood, folk psychology, and libertarian free will

This book has its roots in my thinking during this testing time, but, of course, this is no reason for you to accept my ideas. On the contrary, it is more reasonable to accept ideas that have been examined with a certain degree of dispassion. My reason for telling you this history is that such events are universal. In extremis, we are each forced to examine the bottom line of our existence, and to give such shape and meaning to our lives as we can.

One of the most profound aspects of our strange and beautiful cosmos is that we can experience it, and share these experiences with others. Also – at least so it appears – we can make free choices based on these experiences, and these choices do affect the course of events. Most of these choices are trivial, such as choosing between tea and coffee. Some, however, such as my decision to give the talk at the convention, have the effect of defining who we are as persons, and are our attempts to give structure to the whole future course of our lives. Moreover, such decisions involve us in moral compromises. Trying to advance human understanding is a moral good (even if I fail completely), but it also involved at least sometimes choosing to spend time away from my dying wife.

The example also shows how our higher order choices are

important. Sitting in front of a computer with writer's block is frustrating, and I would be more immediately happy doing something else, such as walking in the sunshine. My long-term wish to write this book makes me content to struggle on. Moreover, there are sometimes severe constraints on our choices, either through circumstances such as illness or because we are prevented by others. I don't believe it is possible to think about these concepts in the abstract. In order to understand them fully as persons, we each need to think about the specifics of our own lives.

What is it, to be a person? I believe that our lives can be summed up by the totality of the experiences we have, and the choices we make in the light of those experiences. If we cannot make choices, then the universe is absurd. Moreover, if we are not the originators of at least some of our choices, then the universe remains absurd. This would be the case if all the decisions we ever took were based on our wishes, but our wishes were out of our control. For example, if all our wishes were completely explicable in terms of our heredity and environment, as many scientists claim, then the choices we make would not genuinely be ours.

Philosophers call the supposed irreducible, radical freedom to make choices that alter the course of events in the world *libertarian free will*. Robert Kane (1998) is the leading advocate of this minority position. He points out vigorously that having *ultimate responsibility* for our actions is a type of freedom worth wanting. Without it, we could not take legitimate credit for our achievements, nor be blamed for our faults. We also need it so that we can be genuinely free to love and be loved by others. David Hodgson (1991), an Australian Supreme Court judge with an abiding and deep interest in the philosophy of the mind, also defends libertarian free will. He argues both for *folk psychology*, in which people's beliefs and desires guide their actions, and also for the necessity of consciousness in weighing and judging between conflicting arguments (see his Chapters 5 and 7). In everyday speech, everyone assumes without reflection that their judgments guide their actions: "I would love to eat the cake you made, but I'm trying to lose weight." To laypersons, the idea that we cannot make genuine choices seems absurd.

I promised, however, to examine everything dispassionately. It is quite possible that the universe might indeed be absurd, and that all of the everyday ideas we have of ourselves as persons are wrong. Science is our best and most reliable source of facts and concepts about the universe. We are, moreover, natural beings, in the sense that we are made of exactly the same ultimate stuff, obeying exactly the same physical laws, as any piece of inanimate matter. Compatibility with science is a compelling requirement for any idea that is to be taken seriously. As Dennett frequently remarks, libertarian free will is not worth wanting if it contradicts science and thus cannot exist.

-oOo-

It is now 2010, and in the intervening seven years I have made several abortive attempts at writing this book. The above introduction was taken from my first attempt. During this time my ideas on consciousness have developed, and at last the book is complete. It is framed as a voyage of discovery from the material world to the sensuous cosmos. The tide is high, and it is now time to set sail from the material world.

-oOo-

Material world

The currently dominant metaphysical position is that of *physicalism*, sometimes called *materialism*. Roughly speaking, physicalism asserts that science can in principle give a complete account of all the entities in our universe. Some entities such as trees, rocks, cats or tables, are given to our immediate experience. Other entities, such as atoms, are posited theoretically, because they help to explain events that we can observe directly, such as the way chemicals combine in fixed proportions.

According to physicalists, simple entities, such as atoms, consist of matter that is completely insentient – lacking mind or consciousness. The consciousness of human beings (and of other sentient creatures) somehow arises from the complex way in which insentient matter is structured within their brains. A human being is, in essence, nothing other than a complex system of atoms obeying physical laws that, given their environment, fully determine its configuration from one moment to the next. This is what a human being objectively, really, actually is.

But human beings also have a subjective side: a mind or consciousness that gives them not-always-reliable, qualitative impressions of the appearances of their surroundings, and an apparent freedom to act. A physicalist theory of mind and consciousness must explain this subjective side in terms of the objective facts about a human being as a physical system. No physicalist theory of mind has found widespread acceptance. One such theory, quite popular because of its initial plausibility, is that primitive mind *emerges* from insentient matter as a creature develops from an insentient embryo into a conscious adult. However, when we try to look at the precise moment of emergence, we see that this proposal, while adequate as a description, uses a comforting word that does not amount to an explanation. I will critically examine emergence and other physicalist theories later, particularly in Chapter 4.

Physicalism has a cultural impact because it privileges the "objective" account of a human as a body or physical machine over the account of a human as a "subjective" being, able to experience the world and make choices. This is seen in the widespread praise of objectivity, often regarded as synonymous with rationality and truth, and in a related condemnation of subjectivity, often equated with unreliable, irrational emotionalism. But criticism of physicalism's cultural impact is irrelevant if it is true. The question arises: Is physicalism true?

Physicalism derives much of its widespread prestige and acceptance as a philosophy because it attempts to ally itself as closely as possible with the rightly highly-regarded discipline of science. Indeed, the two are often regarded as being the same. However, physicalism cannot be identical with science because it is a metaphysical system claiming more comprehensive scope. This can be seen from my earlier sentence, in which the physicalist claims that:

> *Science can in principle give a complete account of all the entities in our universe.*

This is not a statement within science, but is about science. In other words, it is a metaphysical claim. In this book I do not suggest that science is wrong in any way. Instead I attempt to peel physicalist assumptions away from science, and expose their metaphysical character. These assumptions can then be called into question. As a result, some will be retained while others will be modified or rejected.

Navigation chart
Overall, this book defends the concepts of personhood, libertarian free will, and of a cosmos that is – in its very essence – sensuously experiential. Such concepts have been exemplified by my telling some of my recent personal history; but no doubt you can similarly speak of your own life. The book gradually develops a specific alternative metaphysical position that I call *idealist panpsychism*, and shows how, despite its initial counterintuitiveness, this viewpoint is fully consistent with contem-

porary science. By the end of the voyage I hope to have demonstrated how idealist panpsychism is a superior alternative to physicalism, both in reconciling our intuitive, commonsense understanding of ourselves as human persons with the findings of science, and also in clarifying and solving philosophical problems that are beyond the reach of physicalism.

Chapter 2 introduces *consciousness*. It cannot give a complete account, because that would fill a large bookcase. Consciousness here will be understood extremely broadly, in terms of Thomas Nagel's (1979, Chapter 12) definition that an entity is conscious if and only if "there is something that it is like to be" that entity. We will take an approach that fully accepts the reality of experiential qualities such as pain or the visual experience of seeing a rainbow.

Chapter 3 introduces *science* in general terms, explaining how its object and scope have changed throughout its history. With the rise of quantum theory in the twentieth century many prestigious scientists have reluctantly been driven to recognize that current physics can no longer attempt to model the universe independent of human observers. Instead its goals are now perforce limited to collating the experiences of human observers.

Chapter 4 is a detailed philosophical investigation of *existence*. What do we mean when we say that an entity *actually exists*? I consider four definitions of existence, and show that one of them – material existence – is conceptually unclear. As might be expected, this gives rise to problems for the philosophy of physicalism.

Chapter 5 introduces *idealist panpsychism*. This is the doctrine that the universe is comprised of hierarchies of experiential entities (or beings), and nothing else. Even an elementary particle such as an electron is in essence an experiential entity. The name of this theory arises because *panpsychism* is the concept that everything that exists possesses some weak form of consciousness; and *idealism* is the concept that consciousness is the essence of everything, and this essence is more fundamental than physics. Physics does not constitute the essence of an entity. Rather, the physics of an entity describes the veridical appearances that the entity presents to human or other observers. A "toy" dodecahedral universe is given as an example. On first hearing idealist panpsychism sounds implausible, but several eminent philosophers and scientists including Bertrand Russell, Arthur Eddington, Galen Strawson and David Chalmers have entertained similar ideas. There is a final question-and-answer section that attempts to clarify concepts.

Chapter 6 is about **causation**. Understanding how mental causation relates to physical causation has been an intractable problem for many years in the philosophy of consciousness. No physicalist account has come anywhere near to solving it. How does a *feeling* cause a *physical action*? How could the taste of chocolate mousse, *of itself as an experienced taste*, possibly cause you to initiate the physical action of reaching for another spoonful? Physicalists have come up with desperate solutions. A few deny that we have qualitative experiences. Some accept that we have experiences and thoughts but deny that they have any causal effect. Your wish for more chocolate mousse has nothing to do with your arm reaching for another spoonful. Incredibly (literally incredibly) you have no control over any of your actions from birth to death.

Idealist panpsychism gives a lucid, unproblematic account of all forms of causation (mind-body, physical, and mind-mind), and how they mesh neatly together. Moreover, this account has the desirable properties that it is both reductionist in tenor, and is a (non-physicalist) form of mind-brain identity theory. Physicalist mind-brain identity theories fail to explain how a pain can be identical to a brain state when these two things have vastly different properties. Idealist panpsychism gives a straightforward answer to this problem.

This elegant explanation of causation greatly strengthens the theory's plausibility, and it is I believe a cogent reason for regarding idealist panpsychism as a significant advance in our understanding of consciousness.

Chapter 7 is a brief *résumé* of chapters 4, 5 and 6.

Chapter 8 is about *quantum mind*. Previous chapters have already made out a strong case for idealist panpsychism. This chapter begins by asking the question: What do we expect the properties of elementary particles to be if we assume that idealist panpsychism is true? It then shows that these properties have actually been witnessed in the results of quantum experiments, exactly as predicted by idealist panpsychism. The properties are bizarre, and are not predicted by the philosophy of physicalism. The final section of this chapter sketches very incompletely the relationship between idealist panpsychism and quantum mechanics.

Chapter 9 is about the reality of *pain and suffering*. In Europe we are suspicious of emotion. In Ana María's Puerto Rican culture both sorrow and joy are expressed freely. In this chapter I have found it appropriate to express some anger.

Chapter 10 is about *free will*. It attempts to reconcile our commonsense notion that we are the free originators of at least some of our actions (technically that we have *libertarian free will* as defined by Robert Kane (1998)) with our scientific understanding of the world.

Chapter 11, *sensuous cosmos*, marks the end of the voyage, at least so far as my present knowledge allows. It weighs physicalism and idealist panpsychism in the balance, finding in favor of the latter in terms of simplicity, scope of explanatory power, and plausibility. Physicalism has almost universal acceptance today because it is regarded as being synonymous with science. In truth, however, it is a failed philosophical position within which it is demonstrably impossible to explain consciousness, despite taking several unnecessary metaphysical leaps in the dark. Idealist panpsychism also belongs to the domain of philosophy, but the few small metaphysical steps it takes are all soundly grounded in human experience. These steps are the essential, minimal postulates needed in order to give – at least in principle and the foundations of – clear explanations to the multitude of problems that beset the philosophy of consciousness. At present idealist panpsychism is far from complete as a theory – it is more of a framework within which a theory might be fleshed out. There are several promising avenues for progress, and no demonstrable impossibilities that will prevent idealist panpsychism's further development.

Although the current literature on the philosophy of consciousness is vast, only a tiny proportion deals with panpsychism. I give some suggestions for further reading on this topic, and go on to discuss Berkeley's idealism. Some technical points, not covered earlier, are then discussed, including the hard mind-body problem as recently characterized by David Chalmers (1996).

Human beings tend to adopt cultural metaphors and to live by them. As a result, human societies become more like these metaphors, even though they might be inaccurate. The metaphor of physicalism is that the universe is, in essence, a huge machine, and we are merely helpless cogs within it, trapped without choice into following inviolable physical laws. Our hopes and dreams and our perceptions of beauty, good, and evil are "merely subjective": the "objective truth" is the reality of the machine.

The metaphor of the sensuous cosmos is that we are, in essence, spiritual beings, at home in a universe in which all existence comprises spiritual beings of greater or lesser complexity. Indeed, the only coherent meaning that can be given for an entity actually or concretely to exist is for it to be an experiential being. Beauty, good and evil are fundamental realities within this cosmos. The future is open, and human beings have a certain limited freedom to alter the future direction of events on this planet. We can turn it into a heaven or a hell.

Both of these metaphors claim some poetic and literal truth, and both claim to be consistent with current scientific knowledge. By the end of the book I hope to have shown that the sensuous cosmos is the more accurate metaphor, and the far better one to live by. I criticize the inaccurate physicalist metaphor for imposing a nihilistic helplessness on contemporary culture.

Idealist panpsychism is a naturalistic philosophical position with great explanatory powers. By *naturalistic* I mean that one can hold to idealistic panpsychism without belonging to any religious faith. In the final section, I sketch what I see as the proper relationships between science, philosophy, and faith, and suggest how faiths (including secular belief systems) should interact so that we might live in harmony on a small planet. I end by briefly expressing my personal faith.

-oOo-

You are sitting below decks with your fellow goliards of consciousness, drinking stale water and eating ship's biscuits. Suddenly you bite on a piece of grit and break a tooth. Clutching your cheek, you stagger to the cook-surgeon's cabin and tearfully sob out your predicament. Among his many talents he is also a philosopher, and a disciple of Daniel Dennett. He swigs some medicinal brandy and pulls out a large pair of pliers:

"Don't ye fret none. This ain't goin' ter hurt a bit..."

2

Consciousness

Imagine the difference between having a tooth drilled without a local anaesthetic and having it drilled with one. The difference is that the anaesthetic removes the conscious pain – assuming the anaesthetic works!

David Papineau in Papineau and Selina (2000)

Consciousness is impossible to define. I can only point to examples from my own life and assume that you will recognize them by a process of empathy.

Examples of conscious experiences include: The experiences of taste and texture when eating beans on toast: the crispness, sogginess and slightly charred taste of the toast, the light oiliness of the butter, the sweetness of the sauce, and the sticky texture of the beans with their nutty flavor and smooth skins. The experiences of watching a firework display with the fireworks bursting into dazzling flowers of color and disappearing before these impressions can be properly registered; the bangs, crackles and sizzles that accompany these visions, and the thick, sulfurous quality of the smoke. The experience of taking part in a conversation involves using my imagination to understand what my friend is saying; thinking about this and its consequences; and choosing an appropriate reply.

Consciousness is elusive for several reasons:

First, each of us has privileged access to our own experiences. When you are eating beans on toast your experience is immediately "given" to you. I cannot have *your* experiences because *I am not you*, and the same applies to you if our roles are reversed. It seems plausible that our experiences are broadly similar on the basis that we humans are biologically related creatures who use similar language to describe any given situation.

Second, and related to this, is that we are all aware that language is inadequate to fully describe our experiences. We generally agree about which objects in the world are sweet: beans on toast, apples, sugar; but not vinegar, rocks or lemons. We for the most part agree on degrees of sweetness: honey is sweeter than warm milk. But I have no way of explaining to anyone else what I mean by my experienced quality of "sweetness". Do you mean the same when you use this word?

Third, we can be massively deluded about the character of our conscious experiences, as psychologists have confirmed in extensive experiments. For example, we take in far less of the external world visually than subjectively seems to be the case: We have the illusion that we see all our surroundings clearly, somewhat in the manner of a camera. Our eyes, however, are highly directional devices, and the area of sharpest vision is a mere half a degree in diameter. We will miss a huge change in the scene in front of us if our attention is not directly upon that specific detail. There are many other examples.

What is consciousness?

This book attempts to reconcile our scientific understanding of ourselves as biological and physical systems within the world with our commonplace understanding of ourselves as human persons experiencing the world and acting according to those experiences. I am therefore going to be a firm realist about consciousness and experiential qualities (or *qualia*, singular *quale*) such as the experience of seeing the color orange, or the experience of feeling a particular pain, or the experiential

mintiness of toothpaste. I will also regard more complexly structured experiences, such as seeing a toothbrush or a person's face,
as examples of (structured) qualia. We invariably experience a
quale as being structured within a wider experience: never just
blue by itself, but at least a blue blob or a blue spatially-extended
haze.

Substance	Arena	Example Contents	Causation
res extensa ("extended stuff")	Space-time	Matter, forces, fields, Atoms, molecules, Objects, plants, animals, Stars, rocks, toothpaste, lilies, snails, Us (as animals), Flow of time	Mathematical physical laws Blind to future outcomes
res cogitans ("thinking stuff")	Mind	Thoughts, imaginings, memories, Feelings, emotions, Hopes, fears, dreams, Sensations, experiences, Qualities such as pain, Us (as experiential beings), (At least some animals also have experiences) Stream of consciousness	"Free choices" or "Voluntary acts" Mind-body causation Future purposes: *"I put the kettle on to make myself a cup of tea."*

Table 2.1: Introducing the prima facie data of the mind-body
problem

"Consciousness" is an umbrella term that is difficult to define. A
special issue of the *Journal of Consciousness Studies* was devoted
to this topic. Vimal (2009) classified many definitions into two
broad classes or approaches: one taking first-person qualitative
experiences as being fundamental; and the other defining
consciousness in terms of third-person phenomena such as
verbal reports or biological functionality or behavior. The latter
approach is more tractable, but it does not touch upon
consciousness – as this concept is understood in everyday life –
at all. Throughout this book I am taking the former approach.

Table 2.1 is a first impression of what needs to be taken into
account in any theory of consciousness. Ignoring the first
column, it is not intended to favor any particular theory, but
rather to list the (prima facie) data. The problem of

consciousness arises because at first sight there seem to be two different categories of things requiring explanation, having two seemingly irreconcilable modes of causation. How are these categories interrelated? Different theories will give very different answers.

I do not doubt that a human mind has all of the contents indicated loosely in Table 2.1, but this book will define consciousness more broadly. Any entity possessing any mental content whatsoever, perhaps possessing no more than some raw sensation, will be said to be *conscious* and to possess *mind*. This is in line with Thomas Nagel's broad definition that an entity is conscious if and only if "there is something that it is like to be" the entity (1979, page 168).

The role of consciousness

Sometimes, when we are deep in thought, or remembering the past, or imagining the future, or dreaming, our consciousness is unrelated to our immediate surroundings. More typically, however, when we are awake, our conscious experiences represent or concern our surroundings (albeit very imperfectly). Why do we need to be conscious of our surroundings?

First, consciousness is needed for learning new skills. When I was first learning to drive a car, the initial procedures, of starting the engine and controlling the accelerator while gently letting out the clutch, took almost of all my concentrated attention. I was conscious of these things alone, and could take very little heed of what was in the road immediately ahead. (This is a good reason for beginning lessons in a quiet backstreet with an alert instructor.)

Skills once learned tend to become automatic, and only some slight attention is needed for the sole purpose of enabling us to perform them gracefully. I do not have to think about all the separate movements I need to undertake in order to start the car and pull out into traffic. Instead, it takes but a small amount of attention to pull out smoothly and safely. In doing this I am mainly conscious of what is going on in the road, and not of my bodily movements. If one had to think consciously and in detail about every aspect of what one was doing, fluency in driving or in any similar task would be impossible.

Consciousness is also needed in order to provide high level, relevant, holistic knowledge of the current situation when the novel or unexpected happens. For example, if my foot slips from the clutch pedal while changing gear I am alerted to this fact. I must consciously adjust my movements, quickly pushing down on the pedal again, so that I can continue my journey.

The final role of consciousness is in thinking about the future and deciding on future acts. This might be as simple as deciding what to eat for lunch, or as complex as who one intends to marry or whether to change career direction.

How extensive is consciousness?
You know of your own consciousness first, uniquely and directly from your own individual experience. Confidence in the consciousness of other human beings depends on their use of language. You come to trust that others have similar experiences to you because they can describe them similarly, as in the beans on toast example. Human consciousness is complex and involves all the facets shown in Table 2.1, from raw feels, to the ability to reflect, think and imagine, to an individual's stream of consciousness. We believe that human consciousness evolved from more primitive forms of consciousness having fewer features in our hominid ancestors, and develops in each of us throughout the course of infancy.

We are also confident that other higher animals such as apes have a certain consciousness, and the same applies to animals that we live with in intimacy, such as dogs and cats. We form this judgment based on observation of their behavior, but we would be hard pressed to spell out precisely what it was about it that leads to this judgment. The behavior in some empathetic way suggests to us that the animal has a high level, relevant, qualitative and holistic knowledge of its current situation. For example, the excited way a dog's eyes "light up" when it sees you reaching for its lead.

As we go down the phylogenetic scale to less complex animals, our confidence in their consciousness fades away. Can earthworms feel pain? They writhe about and try to escape when we step on them, and so this is suggestive of consciousness, but it is not compelling evidence. The wriggle of the earthworm might just be a reflex. Very simple animals have less need than us to deal with novelty, yet they must appropriately fight or flee or eat or mate according to circumstances. No robot yet created comes anywhere near to achieving the same flexibility or appropriateness of behavior according to circumstances. Must all animals be conscious to a certain extent? Or are they automatons, and we are simply not yet sufficiently skilled at programming robots to imitate this flexibility?

When it comes to plants or inanimate objects, there is nothing about their behavior that suggests they are conscious. We might rationally come to regard them as conscious, however, if we developed a theory that explained human and animal consciousness, and which entailed that all physical objects had an aspect belonging to the arena of mind. Such a theory is called *panpsychism*.

In 1979 Thomas Nagel produced an important argument for panpsychism:

> *If the mental properties of an organism are not implied by any physical properties but must derive from properties of the organism's constituents, then those constituents must have non-physical properties from which the appearance of mental properties follows when the combination is of the right kind. Since any matter can compose an organism, all matter must*

have these properties. And since the same matter can be made into different types of organisms with different types of mental life (of which we have encountered only a tiny sample), it must have properties that imply the appearance of different mental phenomena when the matter is combined in different ways. This would amount to a kind of mental chemistry.

Nagel (1979, page 182)

Cartesian dualism

In the seventeenth century René Descartes devised a highly influential theory of consciousness. He asserted that the universe was comprised of two distinct kinds of ultimate stuff or *substance*. The first was *res extensa* (spatially "extended stuff"), which was his name for what we are now familiar with as physical matter. The second was *res cogitans* ("thinking stuff"), the separate substance of mind or soul. These two substances interacted within the human brain, specifically within the small pineal gland. He had a theory whereby fluid signals traveled along nerves to create a pattern of pressure on the surface of the pineal gland, and this pattern of pressure gave rise to a structured thought. Likewise a thought could create a pattern of pressure on the surface of the pineal gland. William Seager (1999, Chapter 1) has an extensive and accessible discussion of Descartes' ideas. Descartes chose the pineal gland as the seat of consciousness because he thought that it was the only gland within the brain that was centrally located and hence not duplicated within each hemisphere. He also believed that the gland was unique to humans and this was consistent with his belief that non-human animals were essentially unconscious automata.

Descartes' theory has the attraction that there do appear at first sight to be two highly distinct types of ultimate stuff in the universe: matter, such as a chair, a rock, or an atom; and mind-stuff such as thoughts, experiential qualities and emotions. The only common attribute shared by these two substances was the passage of time. Descartes claimed that there was no such thing as the unconscious mind: each of us is by definition aware of everything that is going on in our minds. His surrogate for the unconscious mind was the mechanistic and non-mental physical information processing carried out by the nervous system in the mechanistic or "animalistic" parts of the brain external to the pineal gland; see Seager (1999, pages 4, 10 and 12).

Soon after publication, Descartes was criticized by Princess Elizabeth of Bohemia who wrote, "I have to admit that it would be easier for me to attribute matter and extension to the soul than to attribute to an immaterial thing the capacity to move and be moved by a body," see Cottingham *et al.* (1991, page 220). This was widely seen as a powerful argument against Descartes' ghostly and wholly non-spatial *res cogitans*, and criticism of Cartesian dualism has continued in various forms to this day.

Descartes' theory was fruitful because it allowed for the study of matter without regard to mind. Having thus been freed, physics took wing, and scientists began to study matter in terms of the precise mathematical laws it obeyed. This strategy, initially restricted to inanimate matter, was highly successful. By the twentieth century, scientists also began to regard plants and animals as biological and chemical entities, obeying exactly the same laws as any other object in nature, albeit of immeasurably greater complexity. For most scientists Descartes' thinking-stuff was regarded as superfluous.

The hard problem

Given the success of physics in explaining the world, including animal and human behavior, in terms the behavior of insensate matter, it might be thought that the problem of consciousness was in principle solved. Indeed, behaviorists have argued thus since the beginning of the twentieth century. However, David Chalmers points out that such scientific progress does not touch the essence of consciousness:

Many books and articles on consciousness have appeared in the past few years and one might think that we are making progress. But on a closer look, most of this work leaves the hardest problems about consciousness untouched. Often the work addresses what might be called the "easy" problems of consciousness: How does the brain process environmental stimulations? How does it integrate information? How do we produce reports on internal states? These are important questions, but to answer them is not to solve the hard problem: Why is all this processing accompanied by an experienced inner life?

Chalmers (1996, pages xi – xii)

David Chalmers' so-called "easy" problems are fiendishly difficult (as he himself suggests by his use of quotes), but they are ultimately problems about behavior, and so can at least in principle be approached using the existing methods of science. The hard problem asks: *Why is all this processing accompanied by an experienced inner life* [and not merely a report of an experienced inner life]? For those of us who believe that this is a real question, it constitutes the essence of consciousness. This question cannot be answered solely by the methods of science. Science can only deal with reports of pain and the behavioral effects of pain: it has no way of dealing directly with pain itself (as a real, qualitative experience).

Daniel Robinson (2008) has taken a similar tack. While rejecting the specifics of Descartes' pineal gland solution to the problem of consciousness, and without claiming to propose a theory of his own, Robinson robustly defends Descartes' correctness in setting out the problem (roughly as in Table 2.1). Robinson shows that many modern theoreticians either deny the manifest facts of consciousness, or else they fall into dualism, despite their repudiation of Descartes.

The mind-body problem

Table 2.1 illustrates the mind-body problem, and helps to explain why Descartes' ideas are still influential even though unsatisfactory, and why it has proven so difficult to find a convincing replacement theory.

We know that perceptions and experiences are very closely associated with electrochemical activity in the brain, and that experiences often represent what is going on in our immediate surroundings (I see the desk lamp in front of me). Yet the two rows of Table 2.1 are utterly different. Consider the two **arenas**. All of the physical contents of the universe reside within one, shared physical space (or space-time). In contrast, every human being has a different mind whose contents are hidden from direct observation by other peoples' minds. Consider next the **contents** of these two arenas. Pain and brain activity could hardly be more distinct. Neural firings are distributed in space and have a certain pattern of activation, whereas pain has an intensity and experiential quality ("a dull ache"). A human being regarded as an animal (or just the brain regarded as a physical system) seems utterly different from that same human being regarded as an experiential being or mind or self. **Causation** within the two domains also appears to be very different, at least according to commonly held beliefs. Most academics assume that the popular account of mental causation, in which human beings can make genuine conscious choices, is simply wrong. In contrast, in Chapter 10 I hope to show how free will as popularly conceived is part of the reality that underlies the mathematical laws of physics.

David Chalmers' concept of the "hard problem" puts him in the camp of those who are realists about experiential qualities, or qualia, such as the experience of pain or the experience of blue or the experience of remembering yesterday's lunch. For qualia realists there is a need to reconcile the two rows of Table 2.1 in a way that does justice to the reality of the arena of mind.

Some other theories of consciousness

Cartesian dualism is the starting point for much modern thinking on consciousness, either describing how it should be modified, or explaining how a novel theory overcomes its faults. Usually, in attempting this, a theory will introduce some faults of its own, as Daniel Robinson (2008) shows. Here I will briefly list some general, modern theories of consciousness. Each type of theory will be discussed more thoroughly in later chapters, either to argue against it, or to explain how my own theory is a particular instance of it, but without having the usual weaknesses of this type. My own theory, called *idealist panpsychism*, will be developed over the course of the book.

Many philosophers have argued that the success of science in explaining the causal workings of the world means that consciousness can be no more than an *epiphenomenon*. Consciousness arises in the brain, and is caused by physical events in the brain, but the thoughts and experiences that arise can have no effect on the world. This is wildly inconsistent with our commonsense view of ourselves as causal agents within the world: I really can describe to you the taste of baked beans, and my physical, bodily act of speaking to you really is the result of this qualitative taste that I experience. I will give strong grounds for rejecting epiphenomenalism in Chapter 6.

Some philosophers have gone further and have used the success of science, together with the privacy, inadequacy of language and the sometimes radically illusory character of our conscious experiences to *deny consciousness* altogether. Paul and Patricia Churchland do this, calling their position *eliminative materialism*. Daniel Dennett (1991) notoriously does this more covertly by redefining consciousness in behavioral terms, and then insisting that everyone must speak of consciousness in these terms. Galen Strawson has attacked this position vigorously (2006). The denial argument boils down to the assertion that consciousness is a complete "illusion". Here "illusion" must be understood in some behavioral manner, without any reference to the mind, and this is wildly implausible (as I hope to show in Chapter 9). If the denial of consciousness is true, then people are fundamentally deluded when they talk about their own experiences. It is one thing to say, rightly, that people can be easily and grossly mislead about the details of the contents of their experiences, it is incoherent to assert that they are so massively deluded that they do not in fact have any experiences at all.

Functionalism is the theory that an organism or robot is conscious if and only if it exhibits behaviors X, Y and Z that are sufficiently rich and complex. According to functionalists the entity is conscious *by virtue of the fact* that it can carry out a sophisticated repertoire of behaviors. Furthermore this functionality is wholly explicable in terms of the entity's physical constitution.

This may be understood in two ways. Some functionalists claim that consciousness is *by definition* the ability to perform certain functions. Arbitrarily laying down the law in this way does not solve the problem of consciousness. Each of us knows what it is for us to be in pain, say: pain exists qualitatively as a feeling. A theory of consciousness should deal with pain thus understood, and should tell us how and why it is that a particular entity experiences pain. Such functionalists are eliminativist materialists.

Alternatively, some functionalists claim that in any suitably functioning entity qualitative experiences must (somehow) exist. Why or how this could possibly be so is not explained. Another difficulty with this second approach is that these qualitative experiences can do no causal work, because the functioning of the entity is wholly explicable in terms of its physics. These functionalists are epiphenomenalists.

An attractive theory, at least at first blush, is that of *emergence*. Consciousness emerges from insensate matter both during the course of evolution and during the course of development of some animals, including ourselves. Philip Clayton (2004) is an advocate of this type of theory. Such theories become much less plausible when one tries to think in detail about the very moment when consciousness first emerges. One moment there is nothing, and next there is the glimmer of some real experiential quality. This glimmer, no matter how weak, is an unprecedented, entirely novel occurrence. Emergence theories tend to rely on a false analogy between this ultra-radical, supposed emergence of consciousness and the much weaker concept of the emergence of new types of behavior in physical systems. A detailed critique of emergence theories will be given in Chapter 4.

Identity theories assert that for example a particular pattern of nerve activation just is identical to a particular pattern of pain. The standard problem with such theories is that these two things have very different properties whereas identical things should have identical properties. There is thus an "explanatory gap", and the identity remains a mystery. Idealist panpsychism can be regarded as an unusual, specific form of identity theory, and I will give an explanation as to how it closes the explanatory gap (see the example of the electron in Chapter 7).

Double aspect monism is the term for a general class of theories in which mind and matter (or mind and brain) are two aspects of a single underlying substance or object. The challenges to be faced by such theories are: First, explaining the radical differences between mind and matter noted in Table 2.1. Second, specifying the precise character of the two aspects, the relationship between them, and their relationship to the underlying substance or object. Many forms of double aspect monism fail to meet these challenges. Idealist panpsychism can be regarded as a specific form of double aspect monism that I will argue meets these challenges (again, see the example of the electron in Chapter 7).

Higher order thought (*HOT*) or *higher order experience* (*HOE*) theories state that thoughts or experiences are not conscious in themselves, but become so when we have a higher order thought about them. In other words, thoughts and experiences become conscious when we reflect on them. Similarly some theories of consciousness are *linguistic*, linking consciousness to the ability to use language. These theories may be useful in describing certain aspects of the structure of consciousness in humans (and perhaps in some apes). They do not, however, deal with consciousness as broadly defined here.

Science and consciousness

This chapter has touched briefly on consciousness, concentrating on its philosophical aspects. Human consciousness – the only kind that we know intimately – has many complex features, including self-awareness and language. In this book consciousness and mind are defined more broadly. An entity possessing any mental content whatsoever, perhaps possessing no more than some raw sensation, is said to be *conscious* and to possess *mind*.

In the next chapter we take a look at the scope, power – and limitations – of science. David Chalmers' assertion that consciousness is a "hard problem" is correct in the sense that, as already argued, the problem of consciousness cannot be solved using scientific methods alone. This does not mean that we are helpless in the face of a mystery. We have the ability to reflect upon what science is, and how it informs us about our human nature. With this broader, rational, philosophical approach, we can hope to understand consciousness and its place in the natural order of the world.

3

Science

Today science marches on not so much via proofs as through the persuasive coherence of the picture it presents. What passes for truth in science is a comprehensive pattern of interconnected answers to questions posed to nature... we find scientific explanations credible because they hang together in a finely textured tapestry of connections...

Owen Gingerich (2006, page 95)

Science had its beginnings with the theoretical work of the ancient Greeks, notably Aristotle, but there was an explosive advance at the start of the Renaissance about four hundred years ago, when theory was married to systematic experiment and observation. This is exemplified by Galileo, who, as a student during a mass, reputedly used his pulse to time the swinging of a lamp suspended by a long cable from the high church ceiling. He found that the period of time taken by each swing remained constant, despite the gradual reduction of each swing's size as the lamp slowly came to rest. During its brief history, science has made continued rapidly accelerating progress in explaining the nature of the universe, at scales ranging from the subatomic to the cosmic, and at timescales from the minutest fraction of a second, to the vast span of time from the moment after the big bang, which brought the universe as we know it into existence, to the present day.

Despite this success, and intensive effort over the past two decades during which there have been enormous strides in developing techniques for monitoring the brain and in understanding details of the way it functions, science has made no progress in understanding David Chalmers' "hard problem" of consciousness (1996). There is no explanation as to why we, described as strictly physical systems (composed of molecules, cells, organs, and so on), and moving and behaving according to precise mathematical laws, should actually *feel* pain or emotions, *experience* the touch of another's hands, the sight of a flower, or the smell of new-mown grass. Nor is there any explanation as to how we can also have *thoughts*, reflecting on our *experiences*.

This chapter introduces science, explaining how its object and scope have changed throughout its history. With the rise of quantum theory in the twentieth century many eminent scientists have reluctantly been driven to recognize that current physics can no longer attempt to model the universe independent of human observers. Instead its goals are now perforce limited to collating human experiences. Nonetheless, one might hope that in the future we would be able to give a rational account of the universe as it exists in itself. The chapter ends with a statement of the metaphysical principles that will be used to develop a theory of consciousness over the next three chapters.

Scientific method and scientific progress

Scientists work by using *observation, experiment,* and *theory.* In practice these three elements are interlinked, but a naive account can be given. The scientist observes the world and notices regularities. The scientist then develops a theory to account for these observations. Very often the theory is a mathematical model of the object under investigation. The theory makes predictions about the behavior of the object under different conditions. The scientist performs an experiment to test these predictions and thus (provisionally) confirm or (immediately) refute the theory. An experiment that goes against a theory will immediately refute it, and the scientist will have to devise a new theory, or at least modify it to account for the results. If the experiment goes in accordance with the theory, this only provisionally confirms it, because there is no guarantee that further experiments may later refute the theory. This is why we say that scientific theories are not provable, but are *falsifiable*.

Science is a social activity. In principle, anyone could perform an experiment or devise a theory. This in-principle public-accessibility of science is the essential basis for the claim made on its behalf that it provides impartial, trustworthy knowledge. In practice, however, people rightly have to be thoroughly trained before they are recognized as scientists, and scientific writings are subject to peer review before they are published.

Science is also an iterative activity, in which there is a process of stepwise improvement of the scope and accuracy of theories. At one time it was thought that theories could be proven to be true, but we know now that this is not the case. For over two centuries Newton's laws predicted planetary motion up to the limits of the telescopic accuracy. These same laws explained the tides and behavior of falling bodies and mechanical systems on Earth. Because of this success, scientists were convinced that Newton's theory was true in the sense that it gave a final and accurate account of the character of matter, space and time.

Then, at the end of the nineteenth century, a tiny anomaly was noted in the orbit of the planet Mercury. At first scientists tried to account for this by proposing that the orbit was disturbed by the presence of another planet, very close to the sun. It was even given a name, "Vulcan". This planet was never found. In 1915 Einstein published his general theory of relativity, whose predictions closely matched the motions of the planets, but which explained the anomalous motion of Mercury.

Einstein's theory made other predictions that have been confirmed experimentally, such as the slight bending of light as it passed by the Sun, or subtle changes in the behavior of very accurate clocks. (A clock carried on a trip in an aircraft loses a small fraction of time compared to an identical clock that has remained on the ground.) In general, Einstein and Newton's theories give similar results when speeds and masses are low. When speeds and masses are high, Einstein gives accurate results, while Newton's predictions are wrong. We can therefore say that the scope of Einstein's theory is greater than that of Newton.

On the other hand, Einstein and Newton's theories are *conceptually* vastly different. In Newton's theory, his conceptions of space, time, and of what it is to be a massive object or particle are closely allied to (formalized) commonsense notions. Space is like the three-dimensional geometry described by Euclid in 300 BCE: time flows in the way familiar to everyone; an atom is much like a pebble, only smaller and lighter; and planets follow essentially elliptical orbits. Einstein's theory is far removed from commonsense notions. Space and time cannot be considered separately, but have to be considered together in a curved four-dimensional block, called "spacetime". (This spacetime block is curved in the sense that if you were to try to draw a square in the block, by first drawing three sides, and then drawing the final side, then the final side might be either too long or too short in comparison to the other sides.)

A massive object (such as our Sun) is best modeled as a crease, scored in spacetime. This crease, called the *world line* of the object, extends from the object's past to its future. The Sun's world line is a heavy, near-enough straight crease, which causes a significant distortion in the surrounding region of spacetime.

Planets within our solar system are much less massive than the Sun. Each planet's world line lies along the straightest possible path within spacetime, again extending from past to future. But, because of the distortion of spacetime caused by the Sun, each planet's world line is a spiral crease that passes around the world line of the Sun.

Scientific progress and reality

The example of Newton and Einstein helps us in discussing the philosophical question, "How far can science teach us about the reality of the universe?"

For many years, scientists thought that Newton's theory was so accurate and well supported by experiment and observation that it must be the ultimate and exact truth about the universe. There were a few miniscule anomalies that had yet to be explained, but most scientists were confident that these could be accommodated within the theory. Then along came Einstein, who better fitted the observations by using vastly different concepts.

A natural first reaction to hearing this history might be to say that Newton was eventually found to be mistaken, and that Einstein discovered the truth about the universe. This is simplistic. Newton's concepts hold with an excellent degree of accuracy in the limited domain in which both masses and velocities are low. Within this domain, space can be considered separately from time and is very nearly Euclidian; time can be regarded as flowing uniformly; and so on. When we wish to work outside of this domain, however, Newton's concepts are no longer even approximately valid, and we need to make use of the superior conceptions of Einstein. This is so, for example when we are dealing with cosmology, with very fast particles such as cosmic rays, or with strong gravitational fields such as those associated with black holes.

A more mature reaction is thus to say that Newton's ideas are very nearly correct within their limited domain of applicability, and that Einstein's conceptions are a deeper and more accurate account of reality, and are valid within a much broader range of applicability. (Einstein's theory also works in Newton's domain where speeds and masses are low.) Moreover, we can no longer be so rash as to claim that Einstein or any other physicist has discovered the final truth about the universe.

At the beginning of the twentieth century, it was thought that physics was complete apart from one or two trivial anomalies. Now we know that, even if we arrive at a situation in which physics explains everything there is to know about the world within the limits of our current ability to measure it, then there is nothing to stop a new observation being made that will require a complete rethinking of our concepts. For example, as particle accelerators become ever more powerful, some new particle with wholly unexpected properties might be discovered. Moreover, at the beginning of the twenty-first century, we are currently very far from being in the situation where everything in the world that we have already measured has been explained. We know that present day physics is incomplete.

To return to the question, "How far can science teach us about the reality of the universe?" We can never be certain that physics is complete, and that its domain covers the entirety of the universe. Our observations may be in complete agreement with a theory of physics to within the errors imposed by the limitations of our instruments, but this is only sufficient to show that the theory is approximately valid. There may be some deeper level of truth about the universe that is expressed in entirely different concepts.

Completed physics

Despite this, the question remains: Does a true physics exist for our universe that correctly describes the objects within it and the laws that they obey? This seems to be a meaningful question, even though we could never be certain that we had arrived at this final destination. Most physicists would answer the question in the affirmative, and some philosophers agree, calling the true or ultimate physics *completed physics*. (Physicist David Bohm (1980), however, believes it more plausible that physics never bottoms out. For him, progress in physics is like the peeling away of layers of an infinitely-layered onion, with contrasting entities and laws at each level.) I wish to make use of the idea of completed physics and so it is best to define the concept as clearly as possible.

A *theory of physics* is a mathematical description that more or less accurately predicts (at least in statistical terms) the results of observations made of the universe, either directly from nature (as in observing the stars), or from a specific experiment. This description, moreover, is in terms of the ultimate constituents of the universe insofar as they are currently known.

In this definition, the clause "at least in statistical terms" is needed, because some theories are essentially statistical in character, as we shall see. The final sentence ensures that this is a theory of physics, rather than of, say, chemistry.

Given that it exists, *completed physics* is the theory of physics that perfectly accurately predicts (at least in statistical terms) the outcomes that will be observed in all possible situations – past, present or future – either natural or experimental, by any intelligence, either human or alien. Moreover, this is the theory having the greatest statistical accuracy among those that meet these conditions. The definition of completed physics ensures that it is stated in terms of the ultimate constituents of the universe (without qualification). This is because, by definition, no further experiments could provide novel evidence revealing yet more fundamental entities.

It is impossible to know from any finite set of experiments if any proposed theory of physics is the purported completed physics. We are certain, however, that our present day physics is incomplete because we know of gaps in our current understanding.

It seems far-fetched to me that the physics of our universe is (as David Bohm asserts) like an infinitely-layered onion. This seems too close to the proverbial cosmology in which the Earth is supported on the back of a giant turtle. What is the turtle standing on? The notorious reply is that it's "turtles all the way down" (see Hawking, 1988, page 1). Bohm's picture has the additional implausibility that it proposes a different "creature" at each level. I will be assuming that a completed physics exists for our universe.

Again, for ease of exposition, I will often suppose in the remainder of the book that the ultimate entities of completed physics are elementary particles. Such "particles" have wave-like as well as particle-like aspects. For our purposes, it is of no consequence if the ultimates of completed physics are in fact string-like or membrane-like entities, or if they have some entirely different character. Sentences are easier to understand if we can speak specifically of elementary particles rather than (more correctly and vaguely) of ultimates. Often I will take the electron and the photon as relatively familiar examples. The motivation for these choices is that a very important and comprehensive theory of physics, quantum electrodynamics, involving the electron, the positron and the photon, explains in principle much of what goes on in the world.

Reductionism

Consider a simple mechanical system such as a seesaw comprising a beam with a central pivot. For a first analysis the beam can be considered as continuous and perfectly rigid, so that only rotation around the pivot is considered. A slightly more sophisticated analysis also considers the slight elasticity of the beam, so we can also take into account how it bends under loads or vibrates. Taking things further, we might no longer consider the beam as a continuum, but as comprising vibrating molecules with vast empty spaces between them. We can break down the molecules into atoms and then into elementary particles where (we will assume for the moment) physics ends.

Reductionism is the thesis is that each layer of description (here mechanical, molecular, atomic, elementary particle) is merely an approximate re-description of what is going on in the next level down. So the mechanical behavior of the beam can be explained in terms of is molecular behavior. Its molecular behavior can be explained in terms of the properties of atoms, and these in turn can be explained in terms of the properties of elementary particles. Reductionism asserts that everything can finally be explained in terms of physics. Such a chain of explanation is called a *reductive account* or *reductive explanation*. The simple mechanical description is, in truth, no more than an approximate re-description of what is going on at the level of physics.

Can we give a reductive account of an animal or plant? There is a sequence of biological and physical levels of organization: organism, organs, tissues, cells, molecules, atoms, and elementary particles. For plants and for simple animals the possibility of a reductive explanation seems plausible. A heart is a pump, and once you have explained the detailed workings of the muscles of which it is comprised, the nerve signals coming in, and the fluid dynamics of blood, then there is nothing additional about the heart that remains to be explained. For a simple creature, such as a clam, it is easy to believe that a reductive account might give the complete story.

For human beings, however, reductionism seems fantastical. We know that we have thoughts, experiences, and feelings, and that these influence our actions. In this book we are being realists about experiences and mental causation. We really do have unpleasant and painful feelings called headaches, and these really do cause us to take aspirin. Each of the above levels of organization tells us how matter *behaves*, at a certain level of description, and the behavior of matter, however complex, cannot conceivably amount to the experiential feel of a headache.

Sometimes thinkers reject reductionism and instead evoke the concept of "top-down causation" to explain consciousness. It is true that consciousness seems to evoke holistic behavior in an organism that is somehow appropriate to its situation. So top-down causation has an initial attractiveness. But it has problems:

Top-down causation is mysterious – a law of top-down causation would be totally unlike any law currently known to science. Where does such a strangely "intelligent" law come from? It is hard to explain how a creature could evolve or develop to a state of complexity where top-down causation kicks in, and moreover kicks in appropriately. Top-down causation is a behavioral concept and so cannot of itself explain qualitative feels such as headaches.

There is thus a split between the hard sciences of biology, chemistry, and physics, where reductionism is plausible, and the soft sciences, such as psychology, sociology or medicine, where reductionism is much less plausible. This split arises because the soft sciences use an additional methodology that is unique to them. In addition to theory, observation and experiment, the soft scientist *understands the meaning* of what the subject is saying. Such understanding recognizes the fact that what comes out of a person's mouth is not just vibrating air, but is meaningful language. These meanings include descriptions of real experiences, such as the taste of wine, and real feelings.

Reductionism has huge attractions in unifying the sciences. The universe is one seamless garment, and the sciences should reflect this. When there is a gap – say where some observation in chemistry is unexplained by physics – then this is an obvious area for research. On the other hand, no reductive account has so far succeeded in coming to grips with consciousness. How can a taste of coffee be reduced to neural firings? Chapters 4 through 6 (particularly the latter) will give an analysis of the concepts behind these preliminary intuitions, and will give what I believe to be a satisfactory, essentially reductive account of consciousness.

Quantum physics

So far we have been thinking about *classical theories* of physics. Such theories include Newton's theory of matter and gravitation, Maxwell's laws of electromagnetism, and Einstein's special and general theories of relativity. All are characterized by giving a mathematical model of the universe in which human observers could be more or less abstracted away. Philosophers would characterize classical theories as being *ontological* "concerned with the nature of what is". After an initial period of adjustment, scientists and philosophers came to feel that each of these models gave fresh insights and an unproblematic understanding of the nature of the universe.

The beginning of the twentieth century saw the investigation of the atom and the rise of quantum theory. I do not want to go into the mathematical details of quantum theory. David Hodgson (1991) gives an excellent introduction, as does Roger Penrose (1989). A more advanced text, which is exceptionally clear, but now somewhat out-of-date, is David Bohm (1951). Instead I will give some (not all) of the conceptual features of quantum theory, and attempt to throw some light on them. Quantum theory:

- Was not the product of a single scientist, but was the work of many individuals and independent teams, working to investigate the structure of the atom and of light.
- Is far more mathematically challenging than any of the classical theories – even general relativity. Initially there were two different mathematical models for describing what was going on in physics experiments. Later these models were shown to be equivalent. Today one is still forced to use the mathematically invalid technique of ignoring or cancelling infinities.
- Is vastly more conceptually difficult than any previous theory. Scientists have to wrestle with the meaning of the equations, and continue to argue philosophically about the meaning of their experiments. (Although Einstein had to wrestle philosophically while developing his theories of

relativity, he was completely successful in this. These theories of special and general relativity are conceptually clear.) Even after a century, there is still no consensus as to what quantum theory actually means. Some eminent scientists, for example Richard Feynman, have said that they do not know what the equations mean – they just follow the rules.

- Is the only theory that has longstanding, rival interpretations as to what it might mean. For most of the twentieth century, the dominant interpretation has been one known as the Copenhagen interpretation. It has never succeeded in overcoming other interpretations, such as the Many Worlds and Bohmian interpretations.

Young's slits
An archetypical experiment made famous by Thomas Young illustrates many of the perplexing features of the world described by quantum theory. As shown in Figure 3.1, light is emitted from a source and passes through a pinhole towards an opaque screen with either one or two narrow slits in it. The light continues on its way until it registers on a photographic plate.

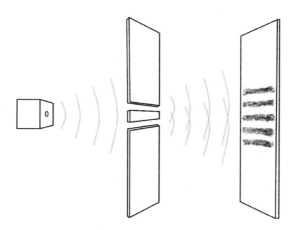

Figure 3.1: The Young's Slits experiment

When only one slit is open, the pattern of light on the photographic plate is a band of light aligned with the slit. The band has a certain width because the light spreads out after passing through the narrow slit, as shown in Figure 3.2. A similar, nearby band is made when only the other slit is open.

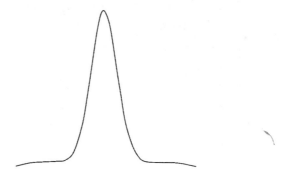

Figure 3.2: Pattern of light intensity when one slit is open

When both slits are open, rather than having two bright bands, one opposite each slit, we obtain the pattern of several bands shown in Figure 3.3. Such a pattern is called an *interference pattern*. Crucially, and mysteriously, there are some regions of the plate that receive less light when both slits are open than when only one is open.

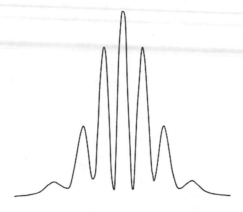

Figure 3.3: Pattern of light intensity when both slits are open

Thomas Young, who performed his experiment at the beginning of the nineteenth century, argued that this proved that light must be in the form of waves. The ripples that passed through the two slits interfered with one another. When the crests of both waves coincided, the light was at a maximum, and when the troughs coincided the light was at a minimum.

The problem of interpreting the experiment arises when we look in more detail as to how the light arrives at the photographic plate, which Young was unable to do. As the experiment proceeds, light is registered on the photographic plate as a sequence of precisely located dots. These dots build up into a pattern of density that eventually form the light and dark stripes. This suggests that light exists in the form of particles called *photons*.

When both slits are open, and when the intensity of the source has been turned down to such an extent that only one photon is within the experimental apparatus at any one time, light still arrives at the photographic plate as localized photons, and yet, astonishingly, the striped interference pattern still builds up.

We can ask some preliminary, naive questions: How can light be both a particle and a wave? How can a small particle, which presumably passes through one slit, "know" that the other slit is open?

Schrödinger's cat

Another archetypical experiment of quantum theory, but a thought experiment rather than a real one, is that of Schrödinger's cat. Here is how Erwin Schrödinger described it in 1935:

One can even set up quite ridiculous cases. A cat is penned up in a steel chamber, along with the following diabolical device (which must be secured against direct interference by the cat);

in a Geiger counter there is a tiny bit of radioactive substance, so small that perhaps in the course of one hour one of the atoms decays, but also, with equal probability, perhaps none; if it happens, the counter tube discharges and through a relay releases a hammer which shatters a small flask of hydrocyanic acid. If one has left this entire system to itself for one hour, one would say that the cat lives if meanwhile no atom has decayed. The first atomic decay would have poisoned it. The Ψ-function of the entire system would express this by having in it the living and the dead cat (pardon the expression) mixed or smeared out in equal parts.

Schrödinger, 1935, quoted in Whitaker (1996, page 234)

What Schrödinger calls the Ψ-function is most commonly nowadays referred to as the *wave function*. In a variant of this experiment the trigger is a single photon that either passes straight through a half-silvered mirror to be harmlessly absorbed by the wall of the chamber, or is reflected by the mirror into a photo-multiplier tube that releases the hammer.

The essence of the problem is that in classical theories equations are always interpreted literally: they describe a mathematical model of what is actually going on in the universe. However, if we try to interpret the equations of quantum theory literally, then the consequence is the absurdity of a cat that is smeared out between living and dead states.

The absurdity can be made even clearer by having a second experimenter wearing a protective suit inside the chamber. This experimenter will see either the hammer strike the flask and the cat die, or the cat will live. In either eventuality, the second experimenter will experience nothing untoward about his own consciousness or behavior. Neither will he experience anything unusual about his situation. He certainly won't see either himself or the cat in a smeared out state. Instead he will observe either one mundane outcome or the other.

Yet wave function that is appropriate for the first experimenter to use, given his position outside of the sealed chamber (let us call this function "Ψ_1"), seems to describe the second experimenter as being smeared out into two states, observing the smeared out cat that is both living and dead.

There are thus difficulties in taking the equations of quantum mechanics literally as describing a model of what is actually going on in the universe. The first experimenter, outside the chamber, has to use a function Ψ_1 that seems to describe the second experimenter as being in a weird smeared out state. Yet the second experimenter is a perfectly good scientist and reliable reporter of his experiences and situation. (Instead of just a single second experimenter we could even put a whole committee of Nobel Laureates inside the chamber to confirm their observations.) Ψ_1 seems to present a grotesque description of the inside of the chamber that is, according to the reliable testimony of a committee of expert witnesses actually present, wholly inaccurate.

The pragmatics of quantum mechanics

In a quantum physics experiment, the apparatus, comprising mirrors, magnets, sources, detectors (perhaps a photographic plate), and so on, are set up in a certain configuration, according to a specification written in a natural language such as English or German. The quantum system under investigation (perhaps a single particle, a pair of particles, or a stream of particles) is represented, in some well-determined way, by what is known as the wave function of the system, usually written as Ψ. From knowledge of the experimental set up, and of the wave function, it is possible to calculate the probability p that a particle will arrive at a particular detector, or in a particular area of a photographic plate. (A photographic plate can be regarded as a two-dimensional array of detectors.) If the experiment is repeated N times, and the particle appears at the detector n times, then if n/N is close to p, then this is evidence in support of quantum theory. In fact, quantum theory is outstandingly successful, and there have been many experiments in many situations that confirm it works with exquisite precision. This paragraph is a précis (I hope accurate) of a more detailed and precise characterization of the pragmatics of quantum physics given by physicist Henry Pierce Stapp (2004a, page 53).

The Copenhagen interpretation

The Copenhagen interpretation says that quantum theory is *instrumentalist*. The theory tells us nothing about the way the world actually is, but only what results we will see when we observe and measure the world. The set up of the apparatus is described classically in a natural language because that is how human beings perceive and understand the world. The wave function Ψ (even though it is sometimes called the quantum "state") does not represent the real state of the system under consideration, but merely our knowledge of it.

In mathematical terms the wave function makes a sudden, global jump whenever an observation is made. If Ψ were a real happening in the world, then this jump, often called "the collapse of the wave function" would be extremely puzzling, if not paradoxical, because it would describe an instantaneous global change in the state of the world. Think of an actual, weirdly smeared-out dead-and-alive cat suddenly transmog(gy)rifying into a dead cat (or into a living one) simply as a result of peeking into a chamber. According to the Copenhagen interpretation, however, this jump is no more than a sudden change in our knowledge, and, understood in this way, is not at all surprising. There is an information-theoretic character to the mathematics of quantum theory that is in keeping with this interpretation.

Another way of talking about the Copenhagen interpretation is to say that it is *epistemological* (concerned with knowledge) in character, in contrast to the previously discussed classical theories, which are all *ontological* (concerned with being). The Copenhagen solution to the Schrödinger's cat paradox is that the first experimenter's wave function for the chamber, Ψ_1, does not model the actual state of the cat or of the people in the chamber (the theory says nothing about this). The wave function merely models his knowledge of this state, based on his current information. A wave function itself is *subjective* in the sense that the appropriate formula to use depends on the observer's current situation and knowledge. For example I had to speak above of "the first experimenter's wave function for the chamber," and not just of "the wave function for the chamber". This subjectivity supports the epistemological character of quantum theory.

In its own terms, that is to say, as an instrumentalist, epistemological theory, the Copenhagen interpretation is unimpeachable. It gives a complete and accurate account of what human beings will see when they observe or measure the world. For this reason, it has been the dominant interpretation of quantum theory throughout the twentieth century. The dominance of the Copenhagen interpretation was cemented at the 1927 Solvay Congress during which quantum theory was subjected to intense philosophical and scientific scrutiny by luminaries such as Bohr, Heisenberg and Einstein. Einstein tried to find fault with the Copenhagen interpretation, but was unable to do so, although his contributions were later to lead to important advances in our understanding of the theory, as we shall see in the discussion of entanglement in Chapter 8.

Stapp quotes Niels Bohr extensively as the leading advocate of the Copenhagen interpretation, emphasizing its epistemological and instrumentalist character, see Stapp (2004a, pages 63-70), and he also includes important correspondence with Heisenberg (pages 75-9). Here is one brief quotation (emphasis added):

In our description of nature the purpose is not to disclose the real essence of phenomena *but only to track down as far as possible relations between the multifold aspects of our* experience.

Bohr, in Stapp (2004a, page 64)

On the other hand, in his descriptions of the Copenhagen interpretation, Niels Bohr sometimes defines measurement in terms of the interaction between a quantum system and a classical apparatus, with no need for any human observer. John Bell remarks on "the inhumanity of it all" (!), see M. Bell *et al.* (Eds.) (2001, page 210). Here, following Stapp, I will understand the Copenhagen interpretation "humanely" as essentially involving the minds and knowledge of observers.

The need for an ontology

By the phrase "an ontology" I mean: "A set of physical or metaphysical principles that will explain what exists in the cosmos." Despite the success of the Copenhagen interpretation, there remains a thirst among scientists to discover an alternative interpretation of quantum physics that will give us an ontology. This is hardly surprising. We know that the universe existed long before we were present within it. Planets, stars, rocks, and water were around long before there was any life. They must have gone about their business, with stars warming the planets and water eroding the rocks, without any help from our watching. The universe, in other words, must have an ontology, and it is craven of us as rational beings not to attempt to find it. John Bell is both witty and trenchant:

The aim remains: to understand the world. To restrict quantum mechanics to be exclusively about piddling laboratory operations is to betray the great enterprise. A serious formulation will not exclude the big world outside the laboratory.

John Bell in M. Bell *et al.* (Eds.) (2001, page 209)

The trouble is, such a formulation has been amazingly difficult to find. The bizarre character of some alternative interpretations of quantum theory demonstrates the difficulty of the search. Here are some examples:

Hugh Everett III, in his "Relative States" theory, popularly called the "Many Worlds" interpretation, considers that the wave function accurately describes the world as it actually is. Whenever a measurement or observation is made, the wave function splits into two (or sometimes more) branches. This has disturbing – but not impossible – consequences. In the Schrödinger's cat experiment, the smeared out cat is alive in one branch and dead in the other. Moreover, the smeared out observers within the chamber watching the cat have two smeared out streams of consciousness – one in which the cat is alive and the other in which it is dead.

The wave function is thus a literal description of what is going on in the world and never collapses. Each copy of a sentient creature is only conscious of what is going on in its own particular branch of the cosmos. The theory is wildly extravagant, but is does account successfully for the observations made by the observers both inside and outside of the chamber in the Schrödinger's cat experiment. Each observer is unaware of their doppelgangers in other branches of the cosmos. The Relative States theory has proven useful in making calculations for cosmology, where we wish to consider the entire universe without regard to any observer external to the system. This very fact that observers can be safely ignored makes this interpretation an unpromising candidate for understanding consciousness.

Physicist Eugene Wigner has an interpretation called "Wigner's Friend". In it both the wave function and its collapse are real. The first conscious being to make an observation causes the collapse of the wave function. This solves the Schrödinger's cat paradox by asserting that a conscious entity within the chamber ("Wigner's Friend") collapsed the wave function, and from that moment on, the observer outside the chamber ("Wigner") is simply operating with out-of-date information. The main problem with this interpretation from our point of view is that it *assumes* consciousness, but does nothing to explain when, where, or how it exists. This theory is thus not a promising starting point in our quest to understand consciousness. The vagueness can be emphasized by asking: Are cats conscious? Could the cat collapse the wave function? Could a computer or robot do this? And so on.

Cosmologist John Wheeler applied Wigner's interpretation to the entire universe, in an interpretation called "The Participatory Universe". He imagined that the entire universe existed in a gigantic quantum wave function until the first conscious life evolved, which then collapsed the universe, creating its evolutionary history. This idea is paradoxical. The conscious life must have been in an uncollapsed state, and yet still have managed to collapse the wave function of the universe. It is extremely unclear, to say the least, what this initial conscious state must have been like. Once again, this is an unpromising approach for anyone wishing to develop a theory of consciousness.

John Wheeler eventually dropped his Participatory Universe theory as being metaphysically extravagant. I believe that we can positively disprove the theory by a straightforward original argument. Evolutionists have argued that the great age of the universe has been essential for the evolution of life, and in particular for conscious life. Evolution takes place by a sequence of tiny random steps, most of which are likely to have been wrong. Under the Participatory Universe theory, however, all possible evolutionary pathways would be taken simultaneously, in superposition. There would be one particular pathway in which, by fabulous chance, everything turned out propitiously for the evolution of consciousness. This lucky pathway would develop consciousness much more rapidly than a "typical" pathway, and the consciousness that developed here would thus be first in the race to collapse the wave function. The end result is that, in the Participatory Universe, conscious life, and indeed all life leading up to it, would develop with extreme rapidity, much more quickly than predicted by evolutionary biologists. Because Wheeler's Participatory Universe theory follows logically from the Wigner's Friend theory, this argument also refutes the latter.

David Bohm developed an interpretation of quantum mechanics in which each particle has a definite deterministic trajectory. There is no experimental way of finding out what this trajectory is, in part because it is governed by what is called the *quantum potential*, and this potential is non-local. This interpretation is of great interest to philosophers because, before Bohm developed it, no one believed that a deterministic account of quantum theory could be given. Bohm's theory has also proven of increasing interest to physicists because, with advances in technology, it has been possible to use computers to calculate and plot possible trajectories in simple cases. David Bohm's writings on consciousness are very interesting, see Bohm (1980), and Bohm and Hiley (1993). As so far explicitly developed, the theory does not yet seem promising as a candidate to explain consciousness because it is too close to turning quantum mechanics into a quasi-classical theory, and such theories, as we shall see in Chapters 6 and 10, do not leave room for mind-body causation.

This is a mere sample of alternative, ontological interpretations of quantum mechanics. All of them have their passionate adherents, but none of them has been widely accepted because all are severely problematic. We can be quite sure that if any unexceptionable ontological interpretation were to be discovered, the thirsty scientists described in the opening paragraph of this section would quickly accept it.

Conceptual foundations

Why is quantum mechanics still the only scientific theory to have rival interpretations, even after eighty years of existence? The answer is that it has never had an intellectually respectable conceptual foundation. Despite the best efforts of great thinkers, there are terms within the theory that remain unclear. According to John Bell, these terms include system, apparatus, environment, microscopic, macroscopic, reversible, irreversible, observable, information and measurement. Attempts of course have been made to resolve these issues, but none of them have been fully adequate. The theory sits like Edgar Allen Poe's crumbling *House of Usher*, above a swamp, with a fissure running from roof to base.

In *Against 'measurement'* (1990) John Bell gives an authoritative, thoroughgoing and detailed exposé of the mathematical and conceptual ambiguities found within even the most scholarly texts on quantum mechanics. His article appears in M. Bell *et al.* (Eds.) (2001, pages 208-15). He describes how the rules of quantum mechanics have to be used "with good taste and discretion picked up from exposure to good examples," and how such rules are specified well enough FAPP, where FAPP is his ironic and caustically disparaging term that means "For All Practical Purposes".

Some university texts try to gloss over problematic foundational issues, or they present "solutions" to these issues as being watertight, when in fact they are inadequate makeshifts. Such texts give the misleading impression that all of the conceptual difficulties of quantum mechanics have finally been cleared up. When a student fails to understand the theory, or how these "solutions" fully solve the difficulties, he or she naturally feels foolish. In my view, the frank statement by John Bell of perplexity despite our best efforts is greatly preferable.

In addition to the wonderful anthology *John S. Bell on the Foundations on Quantum Mechanics*, by M. Bell *et al.* (Eds.) (2001), useful introductory discussions of various interpretations of quantum mechanics and their difficulties may be found in *The Meaning of Quantum Theory* by Jim Baggott (1992), and in *Einstein, Bohr and the Quantum Dilemma* by Andrew Whitaker (1996).

Metaphysical assumptions

This book attempts to give a philosophical account of consciousness that is consistent with contemporary or even completed physics. In order to achieve this within a small compass, we need to make some tentative metaphysical assumptions, and it is desirable to bring these assumptions into the open:

- A completed physics exists for our universe
- This completed physics is of the same general epistemological, instrumentalist character as Copenhagen quantum mechanics

This emphasizes the point, made by the philosopher Kant, that even completed physics can only describe phenomena (literally appearances), rather than noumena (the actualities behind those appearances). Many physicists might object to this, asserting that completed physics must surely have an ontology, and that Copenhagen quantum mechanics lacks this. I hope to show that this supposed weakness is in fact a source of strength. It gives a clue that points towards a natural and appropriate place for consciousness in the world.

- Nonetheless, an ontology does exist for our universe
- A strictly reductive account can be given for everything that exists in our universe

These four points taken together suggest that the ontological level of the universe lies beneath the level of even completed physics.

There is a widespread assumption that *if a completed physics exists for our world it must encompass the whole of reality*. This assumption can be no more than a pious hope given the eighty-year history of quantum theory to date, with the success of the Copenhagen interpretation, and the limitations of all ontological interpretations. I believe this assumption to be mistaken, and that, when adopted – especially when this is done automatically and without question – it is a great barrier to understanding the rightful place of consciousness in the world.

Chapters 4 through 6 will give what I believe to be a satis-factory, essentially reductive account of consciousness, called *idealist panpsychism*. The general idea is that all systems can be reduced to the level of completed physics, but then there is distinct and final ontological level below this, in which consciousness resides. If now or later you find this theory incoherent, please check that you are not making the implicit assumption described in the previous paragraph. I will give detailed arguments in the theory's favor.

4

Existence

What is it that breathes fire into the equations [of physics] *and makes a universe for them to describe? The usual approach of science of constructing a mathematical model cannot answer the questions of why there should be a universe for the model to describe. Why does the universe go to all the bother of existing?*
Stephen Hawking (1988, page 174)

Stephen Hawking's words "breathes fire into the equations" are striking for their poetry. Moreover Hawking does not go on to give an explicit definition of the concept of existence, as one might expect from a cosmologist. Perhaps this is because, as he himself hints, this concept does not fully belong within the domain of science. Rather it belongs within the domain of philosophy.

No one can answer Hawking's "What" or "Why" questions. They are ultimate questions where knowledge ends. Each individual can only give their committed response, whether of religious awe or secular wonder. This chapter undertakes the more modest task of asking, "What do we *mean* when we say that our universe or an object within it actually exists, and how does actual existence go beyond mere mathematical existence, as Hawking affirms?"

The concept of existence is one that you and I have everyday, commonplace notions about. You know that this book that you are reading exists, for example, and that Spiderman does not. Everyone is competent in speaking about existence, but it is a different matter to have a sufficiently clear understanding as to what existence means precisely. Can we define existence? What do scientists mean when they claim that quarks exist? My contention is that even philosophers have insufficient clarity on this fundamental issue.

The phrase "this book *is real*" is used in this chapter as a synonym for "this book *actually exists*". Moreover, when the context is clear, I will sometimes abbreviate the latter phrase to "this book *exists*". It is this concept of the concrete existence of our universe and of the objects within it that I am trying to pin down and capture in what follows.

Four definitions of existence

We begin our analysis by examining four concepts or definitions of existence. These are: 1. *Experiential existence* of minds that possess subjective, qualitative, perceptual states. (We are beings with experiential existence, but there are other, much simpler examples.) 2. *Empirical existence* of external objects that can be inferred by collating the percepts of experiential beings. 3. *Material existence* of entities obeying physical laws without reference to experiential beings. 4. *Mathematical existence*, which is merely a formal description or mathematical model that is logically consistent.

We will ask how each of these concepts of existence measures up to our everyday notion of actual existence. None of these definitions considered individually will be adequate, but several, taken together, will turn out to provide a good candidate to capture the target notion of actual existence. As ever in science or philosophy, the eventual concept we arrive at may be somewhat different from our initial commonsense ideas. The four concepts of existence are summarized in Table 4.1.

Definition of existence	Examples	Claim to existence	Actually exists?
1. Experiential existence	*Minds such as:* *Human mind,* *Earthworm's mind*	Has experiences	$\frac{1}{2}$ ✓
2. Empirical existence	*Rock, Water, Quark,* *Human as animal*	Can be experienced as obeying precise, mathematical, physical laws	$\frac{1}{2}$ ✓
3. Material existence	*Rock, Water, Quark,* *Human as animal,* *Early universe*	Obeys precise, mathematical, physical laws independently of any concept of experience	✗
4. Mathematical existence	*Arithmetic,* *Algebra,* *Dodecahedron*	Logically consistent formal structure	✗

Table 4.1: Definitions of existence

1. Experiential existence

Definition: to *exist experientially* is to exist as a mind that possesses qualia or qualitative experiences. Anything that has experiential existence is called an *experiential being*.

Here, following Searle, Strawson and Chalmers among others, I am taking a realistic view of qualia such as red, pain, and of all qualitative experiences. A *qualitative experience* is a set of qualia structured into a single percept (the qualitative experience of seeing a table for instance, without presupposing its existence). According to this definition it is not necessary for a mind with experiential existence to have any cognitive abilities that enable it to reflect, to know that it exists, or even for it to have any rational thoughts at all.

Talk of a "being" raises a final point. In our language there is a "self" or "being" that "has" a qualitative experience and therefore appears to be distinct from it. If fact, the concept of a qualitative experience is incoherent without some minimal concept of a perceiver, for what is a qualitative experience with no perceiver? To talk of a qualitative experience is to talk of a being that has this experience, but, for the moment, nothing more is assumed to be known about this being.

2. Empirical existence

When several human beings look at a particular rock they will have closely related percepts of it. They can discuss these percepts among themselves. It might be about as big as their fists and shaped like a potato for instance. This agreement is why they can recognize it with reasonable certainty as being a real object, and each can be confident that it is not merely a hallucination that he or she is having.

Science is based on essentially the same intersubjective process of collating human experiences. Early science was concerned with entities that were immediately observable, the mechanics of everyday objects, the flow of water, the motions of the stars, and so on. A major advance came when mathematical laws were found that connected these observations. The observed regularities were now more formal, and could be tested. We can now postulate the (empirical) existence of other entities based on intersubjective regularities in the percepts of experiential beings:

Definition: to *empirically exist* is to have the power to cause (directly or indirectly in any manner) systematic, intersubjectively consistent regularities in the percepts of experiential beings.

An example of an entity with empirical existence is the rock described above. The definition of empirical existence is framed in such a way that it is a characteristic of the putative entity itself, and not of the observers. Empirical existence makes a claim about the rock – it is causing experiences – and this is more than a claim about "what is going on in the minds of the observers". A mirage in the desert is due to the empirical existence of sand, sunlight and hot air. It is not the empirical existence of water, even though the victims of the mirage may believe this.

Another example is the Moon. People looking in a particular direction into the night sky at a particular date and time have very similar experiences of seeing a shiny crescent. The rigorously-comparable character of our experiences leads us to conclude with confidence that there is some external cause of them which we call "the Moon". Examples of intersubjective regularities are: We can study the Moon through telescopes and map its craters. We have a scientific theory describing mathematically how the Moon orbits the Earth, and all our observations agree with this theory. When we do not see the Moon in the expected location, there is always a clear explanation: "It's cloudy tonight."

As I have so far explained it, this definition is anthropocentric. But it is perfectly feasible for alien intelligences, either in our own universe, or in a different universe, to have their own science, and hence their own concept of empirical existence. There can even be empirical existence giving rise to sensation in the absence of sophisticated thought. Consider a group of earthworms passing a jagged rock. The rock, by virtue of its empirical existence, in particular related to its specific shape, will produce a consistent pattern of sensations in the simple minds of the worms.

3. Material existence

Cosmology and physics accurately describe the universe as it was long before the arrival of life, and it seems that the arrival of life (and hence, on the majority view, the arrival of experience) is a contingent fact about our universe. This has given rise to the need for a distinct concept of *material existence* or of *material entities*.

Tentative definition: *Material entities* are spatiotemporal configurations of matter-energy that interact with other material entities according to the mathematical laws of completed physics. Material entities all have *material existence*. Material existence amounts to actual existence, and material entities do not have to be observed in order to exist.

A water molecule is a candidate example of an entity that has material existence. We can safely assume that rain fell and rivers flowed into oceans long before the advent of life on Earth. Current physics seems to give us clear-enough examples of what material existence is – quarks, photons, electrons, spacetime itself, electromagnetic fields, and so on, all have material existence, and completed physics would provide us with a perfect catalogue of material entities, their properties and laws of interaction (perhaps constructed from p-dimensional membrane-like ultimate entities in a spacetime with extra dimensions; or perhaps something different (Hawking, 2001, Chapter 7)).

Physicalism (or materialism) is the philosophical position that takes such material entities as being basic, and asserts that all other existing entities (such as thoughts, or the economy) are dependent upon these material entities). *Ontology* is the study of what exists, and the physicalist philosopher Jeffrey Poland describes the ontological base of physicalism:

> *The physical ontological base is completed by a characterisation of the class of all possible total* [spacetime] *distributions of physical objects and attributes... subject to the constraint that the laws of physics are satisfied... One of these distributions* [W] *will correspond to the current total distribution of such objects and attributes; the others will be alternative total distributions that define the nature and limits of what is physically possible in this world.*
>
> (1994, page 132)

It turns out that, despite its apparent clarity, the concept of material existence is problematic. W gives the current distribution of material entities in our world. Other distributions give alternative (possible but non-realized) distributions of merely-putative material entities. The question is: what distinguishes our actual universe W from its unrealized alternatives? Here are some possibilities:

- Material entities in W are instantiated whereas putative material entities in alternative, merely-possible worlds are not instantiated.

But what does the term "instantiated" mean? In the absence of a definition of this word we have not clarified the concept of material existence.

- Our universe W possesses a real spacetime in which material objects are instantiated (and this is what "instantiation" means), whereas "spacetime" in merely-possible alternative worlds is no more than an abstraction.

But now we have the problem of defining what it is for a spacetime to be real as opposed to being a mere abstraction. This is very similar to the problem of defining instantiation as above; the more so since (in contrast to Newtonian mechanics) general relativity treats spacetime itself as a material object playing a dynamic role in the temporal evolution of a physical system. Misner *et al.* for example speak of general relativity as "geometrodynamics" and explain "the effect of geometry on matter, and the reaction of matter back on geometry" (1973, pages 3, 43). This is most spectacularly observed when gravitational waves in the spacetime geometry are generated by massive, rapidly orbiting binary stars (1973, Chapters 35-37).

The problem of what it means for spacetime to be instantiated is essentially the same as the problem of what it means for a material entity to be instantiated.

- Our universe W possesses actual causation whereas a merely possible world does not.

Here the problem is in defining "actual causation" as opposed to abstract causation. Take the situation in our world where a cue ball strikes a red ball. Putting aside certain doubts raised by philosopher David Hume, the cue ball really does cause the red ball to move. But actual causation depends in part upon the two balls being real objects. (In a mathematical model – a merely possible universe – a cue ball might strike a red ball "causing" it to move, but here the balls, movement and causation, would all be no more than abstractions.) If we do not know what it is for the balls to be real, then we do not know what actual causation is.

We could try to anchor the concept of actual causation by linking it to those instances of causation giving rise to human experiences. (In this book I am not entertaining skeptical doubts about this latter type of causation. Nor am I doubting that science can go some way to providing the links. When I am watching snooker there are indeed balls in the external spatiotemporal world in front of me. Light from these balls enters my eyes and eventually gives rise to my experience.)

John Stuart Mill made this influential suggestion. He defined material objects as being "the permanent possibilities of sensation," (Berkeley, 1996, page xxxv). But tying material existence to causation and then tying causation to human experience makes material existence depend essentially on human experience. Anchoring causation to reality in this way breaks the final clause in our tentative definition: "A material entity exists independently of being observed." Material existence then collapses into empirical existence. This is undesirable to the physicalist for two reasons: (1) the physicalist intends to have a concept of existence that is independent of human existence; (2) it makes human experience more basic than material existence, and this is the opposite of what the physicalist desires for his or her project.

Having a precise definition of material existence is crucial to the project of physicalism because, for the physicalist, the totality of things that materially exist in our universe constitutes the ontological base of everything that exists. The bulk of the rest of this chapter will be devoted to showing that the concept of material existence cannot be modified in such a way to give it a clear and precise definition. If this is the case then physicalism cannot be based on a secure foundation.

So it turns out that, despite its apparent clarity, the concept of material existence is highly problematic. The bulk of the rest of the chapter will be devoted to a critique of the physicalist viewpoint.

4. Mathematical existence

There is no consensus as to the character of mathematical existence, but there have been two major approaches to it that might be of interest to physicalists. (The names of these approaches are my own):

The first, *Platonic realism*, whose advocates include Plato, Roger Penrose, Martin Gardner, and Kurt Gödel, asserts that mathematical objects have an existence in a special abstract realm, which exists independently of the existence of the universe (Penrose, 1989, pages xii, 146-148). Plato, in his parable of the cave, argued that the physical world which we experience is merely the imperfect flickering shadow of the perfect mathematical world.

The second, *pragmatic realism*, asserts that mathematical entities are merely abstractions from observed regularities in our own particular universe. The Christian philosopher Bishop George Berkeley took this pragmatic view (1710, section 12), as did the thoroughgoingly secular popularizer of mathematics Lancelot Hogben. The latter wrote, as part of a polemic against

Plato:

> *This supremacy of the head is very flattering to intellectuals who have no practical problems to occupy them... An educational system which is based on Plato's teaching is apt to trust the teaching of mathematics to people who put the head before the stomach... Naturally this repels healthy people for whom symbols are merely the tools of organised social experience, and attracts those who use symbols to escape from our shadow world in which men battle for the little truth they can secure into a "real" world in which truth seems to be self-evident.*
>
> (Hogben, 1936, page 25)

When we use mathematics to describe "all possible worlds", we are implicitly taking the Platonic realism approach, and are supposing that mathematical existence is ontologically prior to (and somehow deeper or more basic than) the existence of our universe. This is because we are using this discipline to constrain which other worlds might possibly exist.

About these definitions of existence

In these four definitions, I have proceeded from what is known most directly and immediately, and each concept of existence depends upon the previous one:

Mind → other minds → empirical existence →
material existence

This chapter distinguishes between empirical existence and material existence, which are often confused to the great detriment of our understanding. I insist upon this distinction because the two concepts are clearly different. Mind is essential for empirical existence, but is unnecessary for material existence. Physicalists generally conflate empirical existence and material existence, calling both "physical existence". Physicalists need some sort of concept of material existence because they wish, among other things, to explain how mind arrives in a materially existing, initially insentient universe.

We each of us as individuals only know of the existence of our universe indirectly, by way of such experiences of ours that are coherent, lawful and intelligible. These experiences, as experiences, come to us directly and immediately. We know nothing about the universe except by having experiences, and so these should be considered first.

We initially know of objects in the world by observation. Objects make themselves known to us by appearing as regular structures in our experiences: objects cause these experiences. We can confirm that percepts are veridical and not systematic illusions by conferring with other people (minds like our own). By means of this intersubjective process of observation by a community of observers, we come to recognize the empirical existence of objects in the world. It is even the case that we know of the empirical existence of our own bodies in this way.

Our confidence in the empirical existence of objects depends on other minds. This is why empirical existence is placed after other minds in the diagram above. Arthur Eddington expresses this:

> It is true that I have a strong impression of an external world apart from any communication with other conscious beings. But apart from such communication I should have no reason to trust the impression. [He gives vivid dreams as an example.] So long as we have to deal with one consciousness alone, the hypothesis that there is an external world responsible for part of what appears in it is an idle one. All that can be asserted of this external world is a mere duplication of the knowledge that can be much more confidently asserted of the world appearing in consciousness. The hypothesis only becomes

useful when it is the means of bringing together the worlds of many consciousnesses occupying different view-points.

(Eddington, 1928, page 284)

By way of theories of lesser or greater sophistication, we come to some knowledge of objects outside of the range of our direct observation and experience: the Moon when it is behind clouds, the existence of electrons, and so on. But can this theoretical knowledge be developed into a concept of what it means for unobserved entities to exist, as is required by physicalists? I will argue below that we cannot arrive at a satisfactory concept of material existence.

Do any of these four concepts of existence amount to actual existence? My opinions, based on the following reasons, are roughly summarized by the ticks and crosses in Table 4.1 above.

Row 1. Descartes wanted to base philosophy on a foundation of absolute certainty. His procedure was to discard any notion of which there was the slightest question. Whatever remained, he reasoned, must be a certain truth. He argued that his perceptions might be entirely illusory in the sense that it was at least conceivable that the external world might not exist at all. He knew, however, that he thought, and so he concluded that he existed as a thinking being: *cogito ergo sum*.

Cogito ergo sum remains a certain truth even if we reject absolute certainty as the appropriate standard by which to judge metaphysical questions. Similarly, the conditional assertion that *"If X has experiential existence then X actually exists"* remains true whether we accept or reject Descartes' criterion of absolute doubt. (Mathematical objects such as circles provide examples of Xs without experiential existence. Consistent with the assertion, they have formal but not actual existence.)

We know absolutely that we actually exist as minds, but we can be extremely confident that we are not merely disembodied minds, existing in isolation, experiencing the illusion of a non-existent universe. We can be extremely confident that our existence as minds is not all that our actual existence amounts to. For this latter reason, there is a half-tick in the first row of Table 4.1.

Row 2. The definition of empirical existence accurately describes what laypeople and scientists do in coming to the firm conclusion that something "actually exists" (or just "exists"). The Moon provides an explicit example. Each person has a similar experience, perhaps of a bright crescent. These experiences are in such concordance with one another and with scientific knowledge, that we are justly confident in asserting the Moon's actual existence. But there must be more to the Moon's actual existence than its empirical existence. We certainly want to say that the Moon actually exists when clouds obscure the night sky, and that it existed in the distant past, before the arrival of life on this planet. These arguments explain the half-tick in the second row of Table 4.1. (Physicalists would want to say that the Moon continues to materially exist even when humans are not observing it, but I will argue below that no adequate concept of material existence can be given.)

[Row 3 will be discussed extensively after...]

Row 4. A logically consistent formal structure is sufficient for mathematical existence, but mathematical existence does not of itself amount to actual existence. For example, Hawking and Ellis describe several exact solutions to Einstein's field equations, and all of these validly exist as mathematical objects (Hawking and Ellis, 1973, Chapter 5). These mathematical objects are very different from one another in terms of the physical predictions they make, and so it is impossible that all of them are even approximately consistent with what we know about our own universe. For example, part of the De Sitter spacetime is a model for the now discredited Bondi, Gold and Hoyle steady state theory of the universe (Hawking and Ellis, 1973, page 126). We have no reason to believe that there are other universes that instantiate all of these mathematical objects, even approximately. The same applies to any mathematical object whatsoever. This is my reason for placing a cross in the final row of Table 4.1. (Tegmark (2003) disagrees. His contrasting viewpoint will be discussed in the next chapter.)

This completes the explanation for the contents of Table 4.1, except for the cross in the third row, and this I turn to now.

Critiquing physicalism

Physicalist (sometimes called materialist) philosophers, and implicitly most scientists, take the above concepts in a different order. They take entities with material existence as being basic and attempt to derive everything else from this foundation. From the outstanding success of science they argue that we have a clear (or clear enough) idea of what it is for something to materially exist. Current physics gives a provisional catalogue of material (or more broadly physical) entities and their properties, and completed physics would give a perfect list. They can make a mathematical model of the early universe, as it was before the coming of any consciousness, and predict how it will develop. Materialists take the existence of our universe – described in terms of physics – as given, and their task is to explain how minds and qualitative experiences can arise from complex arrangements of previously insentient matter.

This is an extraordinarily hard task, and in this book we are by-and-large ignoring the contributions of those physicalists who "solve" the problem of consciousness by flatly denying the existence of mind and of qualia.

Physicalism is the currently dominant philosophical position about the universe and is thus deserving of a thoroughgoing consideration and critique, even if this is somewhat technical. I believe that what follows demonstrates physicalism to be inadequate as a philosophical position. My positive case for idealist panpsychism continues with the final section of this chapter, and it is possible to skip to there.

Physicalism and material existence defined

We need to examine this viewpoint of physicalism, the currently dominant philosophical position about the universe. Some of its assumptions are:

- Completed physics (even though we might never arrive at it) gives a complete, objective (observer-independent) description of the ontology of the cosmos.
- The ultimate entities of the universe (electrons for example) can be characterized completely in terms of completed physics. Ultimates have no intrinsic, hidden properties. For example, according to physicalists these ultimate constituents are not sentient.
- The same applies to simple entities such as rocks, water, flashes of lightning, and volcanoes.
- The universe, in its initial years, existed entirely without consciousness (construed broadly as any experiential quality).
- Consciousness only exists in small pockets of the universe where life has evolved to a certain degree of complexity.
- Consciousness requires complex structures of matter, such as water, carbon and other chemicals, and can be explained in terms of these complex material structures.

The project of physicalism is to first give an account of material existence, and then to explain consciousness in terms of complex configurations of matter.

A volcano is an example of an entity that has material existence. We can safely assume that lava flowed from volcanoes that spewed sulfurous fumes into the air long before the advent of life on Earth. Most scientists and philosophers would agree that if one had a complete description of the volcano in terms of completed physics, then that is all there is to the volcano.

According to physicalists, in the early years of the universe the entirety of the matter within it was insentient. Today, however, we know that some material objects such as an apple or a mountain can cause some complex systems of matter, namely us, to have experiences. Trivially, matter must have some potential to cause experiences. But from the point of view of physicalism, the fact that matter potentially has empirical existence is useless as an explanation for consciousness. If I asked a physicalist, "How does matter cause consciousness?" and she were to reply, "Matter has the potential to cause consciousness," then I would object, "This is not an explanation but merely a restatement of the question I wish you to answer." Physicalists need a concept of material existence that is independent of the concept of "potential for consciousness".

Above I gave a tentative definition of material existence. This definition could be made somewhat more precise, and details might have to change as physics advanced. Nonetheless, it does capture the essence of material entities and of material existence, as these concepts seem to be intuitively understood by physicalists. I say, "seem to be intuitively understood," because many physicalists don't give any account of material existence before attempting to explain consciousness in terms of complex configurations of matter.

My tentative definition is inadequate because it is circular. Poland's definition of material existence, which he calls the "physical ontological base" (1994, page 132), was also quoted above. It is unsatisfactory because it rests on an unanalyzed concept of spacetime: either spacetime is itself material, in which case the definition is circular; or it is unexplained in which case the material existence is essentially an abstraction, as will become clear. I hope to show below that no satisfactory account of material existence can be given.

The early universe

Some scientific theories such as evolution and cosmology deal with eras before human beings existed. Do physicalism and the above definition of material existence succeed in giving such theories a secure ontological foundation?

Physicalists maintain that consciousness does not appear in the cosmos until the time when life has developed to a certain degree of complexity. Let $\mathbf{U_T}$ be our universe up until the moment before the first glimmer of consciousness appeared.

There is neither experiential existence nor any empirical existence within $\mathbf{U_T}$. There is only material existence. The early universe has a mathematical model U_T. The question arises, "If physicalism is true, how does $\mathbf{U_T}$ differ from this mathematical object U_T?" When you reflect on it, the answer is, "Not at all." Physicalists might claim that the matter in $\mathbf{U_T}$ actually exists whereas the matter in U_T merely has mathematical existence, but the physicalism gives no clue as to what the difference between mathematical existence and actual existence is.

If physicalism is true, our early universe $\mathbf{U_T}$ is *conceptually indistinguishable* from the mathematical object U_T. This conclusion is highly counterintuitive, and most physicalists would deny it, and so it needs to be explained.

First consider our early universe, $\mathbf{U_T}$ (here I will use the convention that everything with material existence will be shown in bold):

1. Let P be the set of mathematical laws of completed physics, which might be deterministic or statistical. P mathematically models the evolution in **time t** of $\mathbf{U_T}$. Within $\mathbf{U_T}$ itself is the **initial state** of the **universe,** defined by the part of $\mathbf{U_T}$ where **t = 0.**

2. P gives a formal mathematical definition of what it is to be a spatiotemporal configuration of matter-energy [a material entity] within $\mathbf{U_T}$. For example P tells us what

water is, and that it is made of **H_2O**. Examining the mathematical structure of a small portion of **U_T**, the laws P might tell us that here rain is falling on a planet for example. This is so despite the fact that there are no observers within **U_T**. **Water**, **H_2O**, **rain**, and **planet** all have material existence.

3. P also gives a formal mathematical definition of what it is to be an ultimate within **U_T**. An **electron** and a **photon** are examples of ultimates within **U_T**. Examining the mathematical structure of a small portion of **U_T**, the laws P might tell us that here an **electron** is absorbing a **photon** for example.

The mathematical model U_T of the early universe has very similar properties. (In this second list, naturalistic-sounding words and phrases such as "time", "H_2O", "planet", "photon", "a spatiotemporal configuration of matter-energy", and so on, are merely labels for specific substructures in the mathematical model):

1. Let P be the set of mathematical laws of completed physics, which might be deterministic or statistical. P mathematically models the evolution in time t of U_T. Within U_T itself is the initial state of the universe, defined by the part of U_T where t = 0.

2. P gives a formal mathematical definition of what it is to be a spatiotemporal configuration of matter-energy within U_T. For example P tells us what water is, and that it is made of H_2O. Examining the mathematical structure of a small portion of U_T, the laws P might tell us that here rain is falling on a planet for example. This is so despite the fact that there are no observers within U_T. Water, H_2O, rain, and planet all have formal existence.

3. P also gives a formal mathematical definition of what it is

to be an ultimate within U_T. An electron and a photon are examples of ultimates within U_T. Examining the mathematical structure of a small portion of U_T, the laws P might tell us that here an electron is absorbing a photon for example.

These 3-point lists are important because they characterize all the statements that can be made about $\mathbf{U_T}$ *and* U_T, *expressed in a mixture of natural language and mathematical terms.* In the first list, I used the convention that everything with material existence was shown in bold. Corresponding items in the second list, which merely have formal mathematical existence, are shown in regular font. The lists are identical, except that some words in the first list are in bold, whereas the same words in the second list are in regular font.

Theorem
If physicalism is true, then our early universe $\mathbf{U_T}$ is conceptually indistinguishable from the mathematical object U_T.

Proof
For every true statement about actual structure in $\mathbf{U_T}$ there is a corresponding true statement about the formal structure within U_T, and vice versa.

For example, if in $\mathbf{U_T}$, "materially existing rain is falling on a materially existing planet," then in U_T, "formally existing rain is falling on a formally existing planet." We can reason in the opposite direction: if we know a fact about U_T, then we know the corresponding fact in $\mathbf{U_T}$.

Other examples are that in $\mathbf{U_T}$, "A material electron absorbs a material photon," whereas in U_T, "A formal electron formally absorbs a formal photon." In $\mathbf{U_T}$, "actual time actually passes," whereas in U_T, "formal time formally passes."

How is material existence distinguishable from (a specific,

corresponding type of) formal existence? The answer is, "It is not." The physical laws P are stated in purely mathematical terms, and the definition of material objects (point 2 of the first list) only makes use of the formal mathematical structure of the early universe $\mathbf{U_T}$. So *this definition is purely mathematical*, and turns out to be exactly the same as the definition of specific, formal substructures within the mathematical model U_T (point 2 of the second list).

The same argument applies to actual ultimates (point 3 of the first list). They are defined solely in terms of the mathematical laws P and the mathematical structure of $\mathbf{U_T}$, and this definition is identical to the definition of formal ultimates (point 3 of the second list).

Similarly, the early universe itself, its initial state, and the flow of time are defined solely in formal, mathematical terms, and these definitions are identical to the corresponding formal concepts of the mathematical model.

We have shown that $\mathbf{U_T}$ and U_T are conceptually identical: For every statement that can be made about $\mathbf{U_T}$ there is an identical statement that can be made about U_T and vice-versa. While the word "existence" in the first case is intended to be "material existence" and in the second case "mathematical existence", physicalists do not explain what it is that distinguishes these two concepts of existence.

If $\mathbf{U_T}$ and U_T are conceptually identical, then they must be identical, for to suppose otherwise is to suppose that there is an ineffable, occult distinction between them. Such distinctions are forbidden to rational thinkers.

(Note that, as already argued earlier, from the point of view of physicalism, to make the contrasting statements that "**Matter in $\mathbf{U_T}$** has the potential to give rise to consciousness", whereas "Matter in U_T does not have the potential to give rise to consciousness" is to make an occult distinction that is useless as an *explanation* of why consciousness arises from $\mathbf{U_T}$ and not from

U_T. It is merely stating what is required to be explained.)
QED

Why does the above theorem work? Can the situation be remedied by defining material existence in terms of different, abstract physical laws? I believe that the answer is fairly clear, "No." Advances in physics might mean that we would have to redefine material existence, perhaps in terms of string theory say, but the argument would go through in exactly the same way. Physics proceeds by means of observation, experiment, discovering mathematical laws, and constructing mathematical models. Once you have abstracted away the experiential beings (the physicists) from this process, all that you are left with is the mathematical model. This is shown in the first 3-point list, where all of the supposed definitions of "material entities", "ultimates", and so on were made in purely mathematical terms. (To the admittedly controversial extent that the quantum character of our universe prevents the human observer being abstracted away from it, physicalism is false because the universe does not exist independently of us. This will be discussed in Chapter 8.)

Consequences for physicalism

We are being realists about qualia such as the taste of double chocolate mouse, or the first glimmer of sensitivity experienced by a primitive creature. According to physicalists, the universe is wholly insentient up until a certain time **T** when it first appears. Some physicalist theories focus on this problem, and these might be called theories of primeval emergence. However, all physicalist theories, if they are to be considered comprehensive, must explain primeval emergence.

If physicalism is true then the emergence of qualia in the early universe is incomprehensible. Insofar as the physicalist project has been developed to date, the early universe is conceptually indistinguishable from a mathematical object. This implies that for any explanation that contemporary physicalists might supply of how consciousness arose in our universe, there would be a corresponding explanation of how consciousness arises in its mathematical model. This is absurd, for it is inconceivable that the slightest glimmer of a qualitative experience, such as a tickle, could emerge from any mathematical object, no matter how complex. (Max Tegmark (2003) bites this gigantic bullet, as will be discussed in the next chapter.)

I believe that the above arguments make the case that, until physicalists can explain what the existence of physical objects amounts to when these objects are unobserved (and the prospects doing this do not appear good), then no physicalist theory will be able to explain the primeval emergence of qualia in the early universe. The failure to give any account of what it is for unobserved matter to exist is, in my opinion, a sign that the metaphysical project of physicalism is in severe difficulties. All of the above justifies the cross in the third row of Table 4.1.

Physicalism remains popular, despite its fatal lack of foundations. The reasons for this seem to be: First, many physicalists are overconfident in their intuitions about matter. Because of this, they do not give any account of what it is for matter to exist, in preparation for their attempts to explain consciousness in terms of complex configurations of matter. Second, there is the widespread misconception that physicalism is a necessary part of our current scientific understanding, rather than being a set of disputable, metaphysical assumptions. Six physicalist assumptions were listed earlier, in the section **Physicalism and material existence defined**. In the theory I will develop here, all six assumptions are false. Most physicalists incorrectly believe that the first assumption is a necessary truth.

Introducing idealist panpsychism
This final section introduces a particular metaphysical theory,

idealist panpsychism, which will be elaborated in subsequent chapters.

Table 4.1 summarizes the four concepts of existence:

- If we know that an entity has experiential existence, that is to say, if we know that it exists as a mind, then we know that it actually exists. But there is more to actual existence than experiential existence because we know (beyond reasonable doubt) that all minds are embodied in some way.
- If we know that an entity has empirical existence, then we know that this entity actually exists, but we know that there is more to an entity than its empirical existence because we know for instance that the Moon continues to exist when it is behind the clouds.
- Concepts of material existence are inadequate. If we assert that there is no more to material existence than obeying the laws of physics, then material existence is merely another name for mathematical existence, and this is insufficient for actual existence. If, as many physicalists do, we extend the concept of material existence by stating that there must also be some potential for causing consciousness, then this extended definition is useless in explaining the primeval emergence of consciousness.
- Mathematical existence does not amount to actual existence.

We still need some rational concept of actual existence whose domain includes the very early universe and its contents, which must undoubtedly have existed in some way. The inadequate concept of material existence needs to be replaced. I am now ready to give the core definitions of idealist panpsychism.

Definition: an *experiential entity* is a unitary entity with both experiential existence and empirical existence.

Definition: To *actually or concretely exist,* (or just *exist* for short) is precisely to be an experiential entity, or to be composed of experiential entities.

This latter definition is explicitly metaphysical. It aims to capture the concept of actual existence, and is therefore supposed to apply to all universes.

Experiential existence and empirical existence invariably occur together in any entity, and it is this unitary co-occurrence that constitutes the entity's existence. In our universe, or indeed in any universe, *to be an experiential entity* is both to possess qualia or qualitative experiences, and also to cause systematic intersubjective regularities in the percepts of other experiential entities.

In brief, an experiential entity is an experiencer that can be experienced by other experiencers. Everything that exists in any universe is – by the very definition of existence – composed of experiential entities. (Anomalies such as Descartes' solipsistic mind are logically conceivable, but do not count as true universes.)

The theory given by these definitions is idealist, because every individual thing that exists is, in essence, a (perhaps exceedingly simple) mind. It is also panpsychist for exactly the same reason, when we note that existent things include the ultimate, elementary entities of completed physics.

Earlier in the chapter there was the fear that, if the Moon's existence amounted to no more than empirical existence, then the Moon would cease to exist when clouds obscured the sky. This fear was reinforced when the alternative concept of material existence proved inadequate. According to idealist panpsychism, however, the Moon's actual existence is a combination of empirical and experiential existence. The countless particles that constitute the Moon are in fact experiential entities that are always experiencing and being experienced by each other. The Moon therefore continues to exist even when clouds obscure the sky, and it used to exist before the coming of life on Earth. Idealist panpsychism is thus thoroughgoingly *realistic* about objects in the universe – despite its idealism. Indeed, this panpsychism's realism is better grounded than that of physicalism, because, unlike the latter, it gives an explicit and adequate definition of what it is for objects to exist.

Experience is fundamental, and was present everywhere in the universe from the beginning of time. The elementary particles of physics are in truth extremely unsophisticated experiential entities. They can combine in hierarchies to form complex, organic experiential entities such as ourselves. Or they can combine in far more stereotypical ways to form experiential entities whose behavior is so dull and predictable that they *appear* to be insentient.

Do these definitions capture well enough our intuitive ideas of actual existence, despite the counterintuitive consequences of both idealism and panpsychism? I would argue, "Yes": They capture the notion of the existence of ourselves as human beings with our unitary existence as both minds and as bodies. They capture the notion of the empirical existence of an item such as this book when it is part of our immediate experience. They also capture the notion of the book's continued existence when it is shut away in a locked room. The task of idealist panpsychism is not to explain experience, because experience is fundamental. Instead, the task is to explain how the physics of the world arises from the interactions of experiential entities, including how mind and body can exist as a unity.

In an argument, very much condensed here, Eddington makes a similar case:

Actuality. *"Knowableness to mind"* is moreover a property *which differentiates the actual world of our experience from imaginary worlds in which the same general laws of nature are supposed to hold true.* [... In an imagined world] *unreal stars emit unreal light which falls on unreal retinas and ultimately reaches unreal brains... Is the brain disturbance translated into consciousness? That will test whether the brain is real or unreal. This property, which is evidently not definable with respect to any of the laws of Nature, we describe as "actuality"...*

(Eddington, 1928, pages 265-6)

5

Idealist Panpsychism

I will try to be as definite as I can as to the glimpse of reality which we seem to have reached. Only I am well aware that in committing myself to details I shall probably blunder... The recent tendencies of science do, I believe, take us to an eminence from which we can look down into the deep waters of philosophy; and if I rashly plunge into them, it is not because I have confidence in my powers of swimming, but to try to show the water is really deep.

To put the conclusion crudely – the stuff of the world is mind-stuff.

Arthur Stanley Eddington (1928, page 276)

Panpsychism

Here are some definitions of panpsychism:

*By **panpsychism** I mean the view that the basic physical constituents of the universe have mental properties, whether or not they are part of living organisms.*

Thomas Nagel (1979, page 181)

***Panpsychism**, the doctrine that the physical world is pervasively psychical, sentient, or conscious (understood as equivalent).*

Cambridge Dictionary of Philosophy
(Second Edition 1999)

These statements define panpsychism in terms of adding consciousness as a pervasive extra ingredient to an already-existing, essentially non-experiential, material world. (The definitions use the word "physical" in the way I am using the word "material" in this book.) The previous chapter showed that the concept of a non-experiential, material world is severely problematic, and so the above definitions lack clarity. In contrast, within idealist panpsychism, as we have already seen, existence is defined solely in terms of experiential entities, thus making mind the essence and bedrock of existence. The physical world can then be securely defined on this firm foundation as a secondary concept, as will be explained here.

The chapter opens with a brief description of an attempt by Max Tegmark to rescue the concept of material existence, giving his example of a dodecahedral universe, and stating why I believe his attempt fails. Max Tegmark's dodecahedron can be adapted to define a conceivable idealist panpsychist universe. This will be studied in some depth. The structure of this putative universe is given both in terms of its physics, and in terms of the minds of its inhabitants. The universe is trivial in its simplicity, but its importance lies in the completeness with which it is described. It explicitly exemplifies and thus clarifies the mind-body relationship.

The chapter ends with a discussion of related views from several philosophers, and with some questions and answers about idealist panpsychism.

Tegmark's physicalism

Max Tegmark is a strong reductionist, believing that everything can be reduced to physics, and that the physics of the world is essentially pure mathematics. For him mathematical existence and physical existence are the same concept. We and the world we live in are nothing but an (incredibly complex) formal mathematical system. There is no intrinsic character to any physical object, and there is no extra fact that distinguishes our instantiated world from its mathematical model: "instantiation" is thus an empty concept for him (Tegmark, 2003, section IVB; Hut *et al.*, 2006, section IIA). His reasons for adopting this position are: the extraordinary success of physical theories that describe the world in mathematical terms; and the lack of any evidence for intrinsic, non-mathematical properties in the external world (Hut *et al.*, 2006, pages 2-3 & 12).

Tegmark's conception of consciousness is that there are (mathematically defined) self-aware substructures in a universe. He goes further and proposes that it might be the case that *all* formal mathematical objects have actual (he says "physical") existence in a Platonic realm. A mathematical dodecahedron, for example, has no more or no less actual existence than the world in which we live:

> *Now suppose that our physical world really is a mathematical structure, and that you are a self-aware substructure within it. In other words, this particular mathematical structure enjoys not only mathematical existence, but physical existence as well. What about* [all other mathematical structures]? *Do they too enjoy physical existence? If not, there would be a fundamental, unexplained ontological asymmetry built into the very heart of reality, splitting mathematical structures into two classes: those with and without physical existence. As a way out of this philosophical conundrum, I have suggested... that complete mathematical democracy holds: that mathematical and physical existence are equivalent, so that all mathematical structures exist physically as well.*

(Tegmark, 2003, p. 14)

Tegmark thus proposes an amazingly wide concept of existence.

A Tegmarkian dodecahedral universe

One elementary example of such a Tegmarkian universe is a dodecahedron, Figure 5.1. The physics of this universe amounts to no more than its geometry. The dodecahedron is composed of an (uncountably) infinite set of points {a, b, c...}, together with a particular distance relationship d(a, b) between any pair of these points. Nothing else needs to be specified. For instance, angles between points can be calculated using the cosine rule. According to Tegmark, this universe actually exists, just as ours does; but it does not contain consciousness because it has no "self-aware substructures."

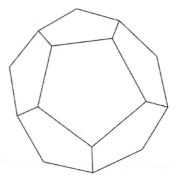

Figure 5.1: A dodecahedron

Critique of Tegmark

Criticisms of Tegmark come under two main headings: plausibility and consciousness.

Several authors criticized Tegmark on the grounds of plausibility, and he has given interesting rebuttals to this accusation. I do not agree with Tegmark's critics on this point because plausibility is subjective and depends upon what one's (at least current) foundational beliefs are. Tegmark's position is a logical consequence of his being unable, given his physicalist assumptions, to arrive at a substantive concept of actual existence or instantiation. As was shown in the previous chapter, any physicalist who claims that physical entities have no intrinsic character and are fully characterized by mathematical laws will be driven into a position very close to Tegmark's. The burden on such physicalists is to explain how they would avoid this.

Tegmark says little about consciousness: "I believe that consciousness is the way information feels when being processed. [...] I am what I am and will continue to enjoy the way I subjectively feel regardless what the underlying explanation turns out to be" (Hut *et al.*, 2006, page 3).

Further criticisms can be made, however. How is information "processed" in a mathematical object? Tegmark defines time formally, but processing seems to require a real flow of time: how does he explain our perceived flow of time from youth to old age? How is there any unity in our conscious experience? The state of our brain at any instant must be a vastly complicated mathematical substructure with many components. Nothing binds these components into a single experience. Another difficulty, made famous by John Searle (1992, pages 214-222), is that mathematical objects are purely syntactical and that syntax has no causal powers.

I suspect that Tegmark would bite a couple of bullets and assert that the flow of time is an illusion and that there is no causation in the universe. But on unity he has severe difficulties: It seems impossible to explain the unity of our experiences; and to deny unity as utterly as his theory requires amounts to denying consciousness altogether (James, 1983, pages 266-268).

Idealist panpsychism
We are now ready to continue the account of idealist panpsychism that was begun in the final section of the previous chapter. Here is a semi-formal definition:

Definition: *idealist panpsychism* is the doctrine that the universe is composed of hierarchies of experiential entities, and of nothing else. These experiential entities can both perceive one another and be perceived.

An *experiential entity*, (which I will occasionally call an *experiential being*), has already been defined as an entity with both experiential existence and empirical existence. That is to say, an experiential entity possesses qualitative experiences, and it causes systematic intersubjective regularities in the percepts of other experiential entities, which are rigorous enough to stand up to scientific examination. Experiential entities are the fundamental entities of idealist panpsychism. All other concepts arise from this basic concept. So the concept of "matter", for example, arises from collating the experiences of these experiential entities; and it is not the case that consciousness or experiential entities arise from matter. Recall from the previous chapter:

Definition: To *actually or concretely exist,* (or just *exist* for short) is precisely to be an experiential entity, or to be composed of experiential entities.

This is a metaphysical statement that defines actual (or concrete) existence, as opposed to mere formal existence. If the definition is acceptable (and no alternative apart from Tegmark's has ever been proposed – as we have seen, most physicalists wrongly take existence as basic and obvious), then all possible universes must be idealist panpsychist in character.

Definition: A *theory of physics* is a set of mathematical rules that collates the experiences and percepts of experiential entities.

The definition of physics given here is thoroughgoingly intersubjective. It is a myth that physics gives an observer-independent, objective view of the world. In contrast to the myth, this definition accurately reflects what physicists actually do, as perceiving and thinking human beings, in arriving at their theories. Physicists observe the world, devise theories, test them with experiments, repeat experiments to confirm the results of scientists in other laboratories, publish their results in peer-reviewed journals, and so on. All this is intersubjective.

Our current, imperfect theories of physics come under this definition, but, as already discussed in Chapter 3, we also hope that there exists a *completed physics* for our universe that completely describes its workings in terms of mathematical laws, even though we might never discover them. Completed physics also comes under this definition. Completed physics, if we accidentally stumbled upon it, would have the properties that it explained in perfect detail all behavior at the level of physics, and also that it would never be disconfirmed, no matter how extensively tested.

If the experiential entities are human beings, then the above definition describes physics as we know it. If we were to have access to the percepts of very simple experiential entities, which exist without cognition, then we could collate their experiences, and arrive at a theory of physics on their behalf. We might have a theoretical model that gave us such access.

Definition: A *universe* is (roughly) a maximal set of causally-connected experiential entities, together with a completed physics that describes the laws of behavior or interrelationships of these entities. The set cannot be extended without breaking the laws of physics. Moreover, these entities are experientially and causally isolated from any other experiential entities.

This definition is approximate because it discusses time and causation in insufficient depth. Causation will be the topic of the next chapter, but I will mention for the moment that causal and experiential connections are closely related. If entity **x** experiences entity **y**, then **y** will typically causally affect **x**'s behavior. Theists would want to deny the final sentence of the definition.

A panpsychic dodecahedral universe

I now wish to give a complete description of a conceivable actual universe in terms of the concepts of idealist panpsychism. This is more than merely a model of a universe, defined solely in terms of abstractions. Rather, it is a conceivable universe, because it is defined in terms of (putative) experiential entities and their percepts. The description of the universe is complete in the sense that both the relationships between these entities (the physics of the universe), and the percepts of each of these entities will be given. The *physics* of this universe will turn out to be identical to Max Tegmark's mathematical dodecahedron, but there similarities end.

First, there follows a brief description that will be expanded upon below. The universe comprises a set of *experiential entities* {**a**, **b**, **c**...}, each of which can experience the others. There is also a *distance relationship* **d(x, y)** between any pair of entities from this set. The distance relationship is such that, for any pair (**x**, **y**) of them, entity **x** experiences a sensation of intensity proportional to $e^{-d(x, y)}$ in the direction of **y**, and vice versa, regardless of any intervening entities. That is to say, the intensity of the percept declines exponentially with distance. There is a one-to-one correspondence between the set of entities {**a**, **b**, **c**...} and the set of points {a, b, c...} of Max Tegmark's dodecahedron such that **d(a, b)** always equals d(a, b) for any **a** and **b**, and so the entities are laid out in the form of a dodecahedron. The above description is not quite in the spirit of idealist panpsychism because it derives the percepts of the experiential entities from the physics of the world (the geometry of the dodecahedron), whereas we wish to derive the physics from the experiential entities and their percepts.

Let us consider, for a general experiential entity, **x**, the percept **P(x)** that belongs to it. In this particular example, the percept is in the form of a sphere, where each point on the sphere represents a given direction r from **x**, and each point is also marked by the intensity of sensation in that direction. The nature of this sensation is left unspecified and unknowable, but we might imagine it as being brightness. The brightness in a given direction increases with the thickness of entities in that direction. More precisely, the intensity of sensation in given direction r is given by $\int_U e^{-r} dr$, where U is the subset of the ray in direction r in which experiential entities are located.

(As an aside, this same definition or rule for determining intensity of sensation in a given direction could also be applied to universes of different shapes. If the universe extends to infinity in a particular direction r from a particular entity **a**, and is completely filled with experiential entities in this direction, then, under this rule, **a** will experience a sensation of maximal intensity 1 in direction r, because $\int_0^\infty e^{-r} \, dr = 1$. If the universe were full of holes, where experiential entities are absent, somewhat like a Swiss cheese, then the set U will comprise several line segments in direction r, where the gaps between the segments mark the locations of the holes.)

Here is a partial analogy. When we look out on a starry night, the stars seem to be fixed to a sphere, called the *celestial sphere*. We experience different brightness in each direction, depending on where the stars are located. In reality, the stars are at vastly different distances from us; some may be 10 light-years away, and some may be many thousands of light-years away, and so on, and so the celestial sphere is not a literal sphere in space, as was believed by early astronomers, but is rather a sphere of directions. The percept, **P(x)**, of entity **x** is like the celestial sphere, in that it is a sphere of directions, marked by brightness in each direction. There are some points of disanalogy between looking at the night sky and this particular example:

- We can only take in a limited amount of the night sky at a time, whereas the experiential entities are supposed to be able to perceive in all directions simultaneously.
- The stars are of different and finite brightness, whereas the experiential entities are all of equal, infinitesimal brightness.
- The stars are scattered discretely in space, whereas the experiential entities exist in a continuum.
- If two stars are lined up behind one another, then the further star is blocked from sight, whereas intervening experiential entities do not prevent those behind them from being perceived.

The entity at the center of the dodecahedron will have a symmetrical percept in which the perceived faces of the dodecahedron brighten slightly towards the edges, and where the vertices are brightest of all. An entity that lies towards one of the faces of the dodecahedron will "see" this face filling a larger part of its perceptual field, and as being fainter than the opposite, more distant faces. More formally, each entity's perceptual field has a particular mathematical structure, given by the above exponential decline rule. For each entity, there is a particular, calculable total intensity of perception in each direction.

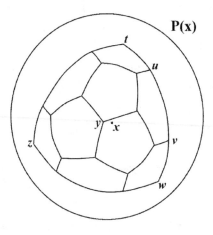

Figure 5.2: A percept or, more precisely, the mathematical structure abstracted from the percept of an experiential entity

I have tried to sketch the percept of one such entity in Figure 5.2. The sphere $P(x)$ represents the percept or mind of experiential entity x, which happens to lie at one of the vertices of the dodecahedron. We can regard the center of the sphere, labeled x, as being x's point of view. The only part of the percept with intensity greater than zero lies within the spherical triangle twz, in which x is "looking within or towards" the dodecahedron. The arc tuvw is x's percept of one of the three faces adjacent to it, namely the face with corners tuvwx. This face is experienced as an arc because it is "seen" edge-on. Points u and v are the points of most intense sensation along arc tuvw. Point y on the sphere is x's perception in the direction towards the opposite vertex y of the dodecahedron. It is the point of most intense sensation of all, because x is "looking through" and experiencing the entire diameter of the dodecahedron.

This dodecahedral universe is actual or concrete or real in the same strong sense that our own universe is real. It is not merely a mathematical abstraction. In more detail, each entity x in the universe has an experiential existence. There is "something it is like to be" that entity. Although entity x cannot think, it does have a percept, $P(x)$, and, moreover this perception is veridical, in that it accurately reflects x's position in the dodecahedron. Modeling Descartes' argument, we can say on behalf of such an entity, "It perceives, therefore it is."

The physics of this universe is given by the mathematical model of the dodecahedron. Although there are no physicists in this universe, there are a multitude of observers. We might whimsically imagine them as astronomers looking out on their tiny universe. A particular entity a is examined by all of the other entities in the dodecahedron. From the viewpoint each of these others, a is just a perceptual speck of a certain magnitude in a certain direction. These percepts can be collated to place a at a certain point in the dodecahedron. As viewed by the others, a is just a point. Just as in our universe, a's percept is private, and the other entities have no access to it.

Strict idealist panpsychism

In the above account, I have been somewhat anthropocentric about the experiential beings in the dodecahedral universe, and I have also introduced the physics of the universe early in the discussion. But it is one of the principles of idealist panpsychism that experiential entities, their percepts and interrelationships constitute the fundamental facts of the universe, and that the physics of the universe is a secondary formal description of these fundamental facts.

What should I do in order to present this example in strict accordance with this principle? The argument would have to be somewhat as follows:

This particular idealist panpsychist universe is a given set of experiential entities, {a, b, c...}, together with their corresponding percepts, {P(a), P(b), P(c)...}. These percepts are supposed to have some experiential quality, but we do not know what this is. These facts are all that is given about this particular universe.

There is no concept of time in this example universe, and the minds of these experiential entities comprise only their individual percepts. They have no powers of cognition and so they cannot reflect upon their observations; nor do they have any means of communication. Such entities cannot develop a theory of physics for themselves. Nonetheless, from the information above, we can collate their percepts on their behalf to work out a well-defined physics.

Taking a sample of percepts, we can plot their structure as spheres of intensity, perhaps using a computer with a graphical display. We would be able to see for ourselves the dodecahedral character of these percepts. There would be one and only one percept from the entire set which was symmetrical in the sense that twenty symmetrically placed locations on the sphere had identical and greatest intensity, and the arcs joining these locations were more intense than nearby points. We might speculate that this percept belonged to the entity at the center of a dodecahedron, where the twenty locations of maximal intensity were the vertices of the dodecahedron, and the arcs were the edges.

Given this symmetrical percept alone, there many other candidate shapes for the universe. Most candidates would be rather like dodecahedra, but with convex or concave rather than planar faces. However, we could examine the set of percepts and find exactly twenty in which the intensity of the percept was zero except within a spherical triangle, as sketched in Figure 5.2. We could speculate that these twenty percepts belonged to the entities at the vertices of a dodecahedron. By examining these percepts, as already discussed, we might conclude that perceived arc tuvw might represent the planar face tuvwx of a dodecahedron as perceived edge-on. Using similar evidence we would be strengthened in our belief that the universe was in the shape of a dodecahedron, and we could state this belief as a formal hypothesis.

We may then, by examining the detailed pattern of intensities of the percepts of the experiential entities, particularly the one in the center and those forming the vertices, attempt to discover the rule governing the distance apart of these entities. Hopefully, we would quickly arrive at a proposed law of physics where distance is defined in terms of intensity of perception:

Proposed law of physics (definition of distance): if, for any pair of entities x, y, entity x experiences a sensation of infinitesimal intensity $e^{-D}\, dr$, in the direction r, caused by y, then the *distance* $d(x, y)$ between x and y is defined to be D.

Using the complete set of entities and their percepts we could check that this law was consistent with all of the entities forming a dodecahedron, thus confirming the hypothesis. We could safely conclude that this physics (which in this very elementary example, reduces to geometry) is true of this world because it accurately and consistently reflects the percepts of all the entities in the world.

Thus, at least for this rudimentary example, we can derive the physics from the elementary entities and their percepts. It is much more difficult to try to do the same for our universe. We initially have only a very partial knowledge of the percepts of only a few of the most complex entities – ourselves. We would have to guess at laws determining what the percepts of the ultimate constituents of physics might be, and how these ultimates might combine lawfully into composite experiential entities. The geometry of the universe and the laws of physics are much more complicated. There is a concept of time in which the entities interact in complex ways, and with only partial information about each other. Nonetheless, this example demonstrates in principle how idealist panpsychism can work.

Mind, body, and world

The dodecahedral example also demonstrates the principles by which mind, body, and the physics of the world are interrelated.

First, the world is idealist because it is composed of experiential entities, which are in essence minds, and of nothing else. In this example the entities are not organized into hierarchies, but in more complex examples they might be. Second, the physics of this world is derived by collating the percepts of the experiential entities within it. This is just the same way that laws of physics are discovered in our world. Third, this world is panpsychic because every physical object within it (every object of intersubjective experience) is also an experiential entity.

The idealist panpsychic dodecahedral world has a mathematical model. This comprises a dodecahedron, together with a sphere associated with each point of the dodecahedron, and with a positive or zero number (representing intensity) associated with each point on the surface of each sphere. Does this entire mathematical model constitute the physics of this world? No. The physics of the world is just the dodecahedron, because each experiential entity within the world has a percept of a dodecahedron, and of nothing else.

Each entity x in this simple world has a percept $P(x)$, and, in this example, this percept constitutes the entirety of the mind of x. There are still, however, some analogies between minds in this simple world, and minds in our world:

- Each mind in the simple world is hidden, and it cannot be observed by other entities within the world using the methods of physics. The same applies in our world.
- Each mind in the simple world is associated with its physical body. In the simple world this body is perceived by the other entities in the world as no more than a point on the dodecahedron. In our world, each (human) mind is associated with a physical body that is located in space in a very small region, say of the order of one cubic meter. What is more, other humans can see or examine no more than this physical body.
- Minds in the simple world are perspectival, and the perspective they have on the world is closely associated with the positions of their physical bodies in the world. The same applies in our world.

For example, when I have the experience of seeing the interior of Blackwell's coffee shop in Oxford, I see my hands in front of me, and my reflection in the mirror. My companions also experience seeing my body in this same location. My mind thus has a perspectival view of the universe that is closely linked with the position of my body in the universe.

Because the dodecahedral example is so elementary, it throws light on the way in which mind and body are interrelated in our universe. For each experiential entity, x, considered as a whole, we can clearly see the relationship between it and its various aspects: (1) its location as perceived by others within the dodecahedron; (2) its qualitative percept, $P(x)$, of the dodecahedron; and (3) its center of perspective, which is the central point of the sphere $P(x)$. We can also see the distinction between (4) *mind* in the abstract, where sphere $P(\ )$ is the arena in which the intensity at each point could in principle take on any nonnegative value; and (2 again) the *contents of mind*, which is a particular percept, $P(x)$, giving particular values of intensity to each point on the surface of the sphere.

In a more complex example, where the universe possessed a concept of time, there could also be additional aspects to **x**: (5) its memory of past experiences; and (6) its choices for future action based on its memory and its percept.

As we have seen from the example, an experiential entity, **x**, is constituted entirely by these bound-together aspects. There is nothing to **x** in addition to these aspects, nor is there anything "underlying" them. In particular there is no underlying material sensory apparatus. The entity **x** just has the raw ability to perceive its surroundings.

According to idealist panpsychism, in our universe, the ultimates of physics have this same general character and raw ability. Human beings have sensory apparatus, but these are composed of hierarchies of experiential beings that signal some part of their percepts to one another. The percepts of ultimates are veridical, but humans can be deceived in their perceptions because of signaling errors in or errors in interpreting their indirect and complex percepts.

We can also see from the example that because the percept is structured, it contains implicit knowledge, even though the primitive entity cannot think. Thus there might be implicit knowledge that the intensity in one direction was twice the intensity in a second direction; that the angle between these directions has a particular size; and so on. If there were no such implicit knowledge, then the structure of the percept might as well not exist.

Categorizing idealist panpsychism

Idealist panpsychism is a specific kind of *identity theory*. Every individual thing that exists is, as a matter of fact (or in essence), an experiential entity, or mind. An experiential entity's physical properties are just a formal description of how it appears to other experiential entities that are observing it. Physics (even completed physics) is solely about the structure of appearances, and can tell us nothing about what a physical object is in and of itself. These two different viewpoints – of an experiential entity as it is in itself, and of this exact same entity as it appears to others – explain how a single entity can have two different categories of properties. This is illustrated in the dodecahedral example, where each entity is perceived in terms of its physics as nothing more than a point.

This entity has two broad aspects. First, and most important, is its essential *experiential existence* as a mind. This mind is complex and can itself be subdivided into aspects, listed as (2) through (6) in the previous section. Second, (listed as (1) in the previous section) is its *physical existence*, or body. Recall that, in idealist panpsychism, the physical existence of an experiential entity is precisely its causing systematic percepts in other experiential beings.

Contrasting the dodecahedral universes

We may sum up by contrasting Max Tegmark's dodecahedral universe with the dodecahedral universe of idealist panpsychism.

Max Tegmark's universe is a mere abstraction. Its existence is mathematical existence and nothing more. Even if we were to label the points of Tegmark's universe "material" points, this label would be empty of meaning.

It is wrong to think of the idealist panpsychic universe as comprising "material" points arranged in the form of a dodecahedron, with perceptions tacked on as an afterthought. Rather, it comprises entities, whose minds constitute the essence of what they are. These experiential entities are interrelated in a coherent way, definable in terms of their perceptions, and it is this intersubjectivity that gives rise to a mathematically describable physics. Physics thus arises from sentience, and not the other way round. With this idealist panpsychic universe it is coherent to ask whether or not it actually exists, because, despite its much greater simplicity, the character of its existence is the same as that of our own universe.

Could these universes exist? Proposing the existence of a universe of experiential entities is a bolder step than proposing that a mathematical object exists "as a real universe" in some unspecified manner. The idealist panpsychic universe is logically consistent, and so it might conceivably exist, although there is no way of verifying this. The existence of Max Tegmark's universe is equally unverifiable, but it has the additional problem that it is unclear what the existence of this universe might mean, over and above mathematical existence.

The scope of idealist panpsychism

The dodecahedral universe is very much a "toy" example for exploring idealist panpsychism. The philosophy has a much wider scope, and there are many conceivable worlds conforming to its principles, ranging in complexity right up to our own.

The rule that states how each entity perceives another (in our example, that entity x feels a sensation of intensity proportional to $e^{-d(x, y)}$ in the direction of entity y, and vice versa) is an example of what David Chalmers (2006, pages 127-9) calls a *psychophysical law*, relating the phenomenal with the physical worlds.

Other psychophysical laws are of course possible, and I am not suggesting that the perceptual space in the toy example resembles that of any entity in our own universe. The perceptual space of an entity x would probably not be in the form of a sphere, but instead have some different mathematical structure. The rules for determining the particular percept could have any degree of complexity. In short, the structure of x's percept could be described mathematically in almost any way.

Again, the physics of the world are far more complicated, for example including the concepts of causality and time, and laws of motion. Time also allows for entities with memories and choices of actions. The thesis of this book is that our own universe is an example of an idealist panpsychist world.

Philosophical viewpoints

Philosophers throughout the ages have had theories about the relationship between mind and the physical world that are relevant to the ideas presented here.

Bishop George Berkeley developed the philosophy of idealism in *Principles of Human Knowledge* (1710), and in *Three Dialogues* (1734). *Idealism* is the philosophy that mind is primary, and that the (perhaps merely apparent) objects of commonplace experience must be explained in terms of mind. He begins his *Principles* (emphasis in the original):

> *It is evident to anyone who takes a survey of the objects of human knowledge, that they are either ideas actually imprinted on our senses, or else such as are perceived by attending to the passions and operations of the mind...*
>
> *But besides all that endless variety of ideas or objects of knowledge, there is likewise something which knows or perceives them, and exercises divers operations, as willing, imagining, remembering about them. This perceiving active being is what I call* mind, spirit, soul *or* myself.
>
> George Berkeley (1996, page 24)

Rather than taking the panpsychic route of supposing that an object of experience, an apple for example, comprises hierarchies of experiential entities, Berkeley instead supposed that the apple resided as an idea in the Mind of God. Critics claimed that this meant that the apple was no more than an illusion, but, for Berkeley, the Mind of God was the most Real and Certain place conceivable. Berkeley is frequently dismissed in a sentence or two, citing Samuel Johnson's fatuous kicking of a stone: "I refute him thus!" Berkeley, however, is still worthy of study, particularly in his critique of the abstract concept of "matter". His definition "esse est percipi" ("*To be* is to be perceived") is half of the definition of existence given by idealist panpsychism.

In his *Critique of Pure Reason* (1781), Kant contrasted the *phenomena* – the appearances that the world presents to us through our senses – with the *noumena* – the realities giving rise to these phenomena. He claimed that the phenomena were all that were accessible to us either through common experience or through science. The noumena were forever unknowable. This echoed Plato's allegory of the cave, where the chained inhabitants could only see shadows on the wall (the phenomena), and were without access to the realities that cast those shadows (the noumena).

Russell, Eddington, Strawson and Chalmers have pointed out the chink whereby, in the case of ourselves, we know the noumenon. As Eddington puts it in *The Nature of the Physical World* (emphasis in the original):

> *In science we study the linkage of pointer readings with pointer readings...* There is nothing to prevent the assemblage of atoms constituting a brain from being of itself a thinking object in virtue of that nature which physics leaves undetermined and undeterminable. *If we must embed our indicator readings in some kind of background, at least let us accept the only hint we have received as to the significance of the background – namely that it has a nature capable of manifesting itself as mental activity.*
>
> Arthur Stanley Eddington (1928, page 260)

Galen Strawson has discussed Eddington's argument more extensively in a paper, *Realistic Monism: Why Physicalism Entails Panpsychism* (2006). David Chalmers argues thusly:

There is only one class of intrinsic, nonrelational property with which we have any direct familiarity, and this is the class of phenomenal properties. It is natural to speculate that there may be some relation or even overlap between the uncharacterised intrinsic properties of physical entities, and the familiar intrinsic properties of experience. Perhaps, as Russell suggested, at least some of the intrinsic properties of the physical are themselves a variety of phenomenal property? The idea sounds wild at first, but on reflection it becomes less so. After all, we really have no idea about the intrinsic properties of the physical. Their nature is up for grabs, and phenomenal properties seem as likely a candidate as any other.

There is of course the threat of panpsychism. I am not so sure that this is such a bad prospect ...

David Chalmers (1996, pages 153-4)

So, in contrast to Kant, the later philosophers Eddington, Russell, Strawson and Chalmers claim to know (or are at least able to make a reasoned hypothesis about) the noumenon. In other words, they have found the beginnings of a way to escape from Plato's cave!

Some questions and answers about idealist panpsychism

Q: How can experiential entities be the fundamental objects of the cosmos? Aren't they too complicated, comprising as they do the six different aspects that you listed, including a structured percept and a location in space?

A: An electron is currently regarded as a fundamental particle despite the fact that it possesses the features of mass, charge, spin orientation and (at least approximately) momentum and location in space. So possessing multiple features does not preclude an entity from being fundamental.

Q: But an experiential entity is a tiny mind. Doesn't mind require grounding in matter, or at least in some kind of "substance"?

A: My thesis is no: experiential entities exist in and of themselves, in communities with other experiential entities. They are fundamental and thus require no grounding in matter, "substance" or anything else.

Q: But isn't physics by definition the bottom level of existence? How do these experiential entities exist at a level below that of physics?

A: As we saw in previous chapters, physics proceeds by collating the experiences of experiential entities (namely us), and systematic regularities among these experiences are regarded as being physically real. So – *because this is the way that human beings actually do physics* – the concept of being physically real depends upon the fundamental concept of being an experiential entity. In our universe cosmology gives us good reason to believe that entities of some sort existed long before the advent of life. The hypothesis of idealist panpsychism is that all such entities are experiential entities.

Q: Doesn't idealist panpsychism turn appearance and reality upside down?

A: Yes. According materialism, the entities described by physics actually exist, and minds just show the appearance of this reality. In idealist panpsychism, minds are what actually exist, and physics describes the veridical appearances of minds to other minds.

Q: If, in your example, an experiential entity is a physical point, then where is its sphere of percepts located?

A: This question implicitly makes the materialist assumption that physics is the fundamental level of existence, and so the perceptual space must be located somewhere within physical space. In the example the experiential entity is actually a mind with a spherical percept that appears to other minds as a physical point. There is no *a priori* reason why a mind with any structure cannot appear to other minds as having any form whatsoever.

A related question may be posed for humans. When someone is looking at the Moon, where is their percept of the Moon, if their brain is physically just a collection of neurons? This is a paradox for physicalists, but can be solved in principle by idealist panpsychism, as the dodecahedral example shows.

Q: How does idealist panpsychism differ from other forms of panpsychism?

A: Once I was at a conference where someone explained panpsychism by claiming that mind was another fundamental physical property "like mass or charge". I initially thought this was a wonderful idea, but later came to have doubts. Physicists would rightly protest that conventional properties such as mass and charge fully explained the behavior of elementary particles: there was no sign of additional mind-like properties. In contrast, idealist panpsychism states that the entities studied by physicists simply are – as a matter of fact and in essence – experiential entities. The dodecahedral example shows how perceptual states are hidden from scrutiny by others.

Q: Doesn't this mean that idealist panpsychism is just metaphysical, with no consequences for physics?

A: Idealist panpsychism has no consequences for physics, and so it does not contradict physics. It does have consequences for philosophy and for science in general:

- It gives a far clearer picture of what it means for the universe and entities within it to exist, as we have seen in this and the previous chapter.
- It gives a far greater hope that we can solve the mind-matter problem in a natural way. The problem is no longer philosophically hard. Although each step would be fiendishly difficult, we could in principle: (1) develop a theory of the percepts possessed by the ultimate entities of physics; (2) develop a theory of how percepts amalgamated as these ultimates combined; (3) compare this

model of amalgamated consciousness with the reported human stream of consciousness.

Q: Isn't your idealist panpsychic dodecahedral universe just another (more complicated) mathematical model? Hence it is vulnerable to the criticism that mathematical existence does not amount to actual existence.

A: No. The entities comprising the universe are, *by supposition*, experiential entities, possessing actual qualitative percepts. We cannot know what these experiential qualities are, only how they are structured. The very fact that these qualities are assumed to exist ensures that these experiential beings, and the universe they constitute, are not mere mathematical abstractions.

Q: What about time and causality?

A: These subjects will be considered in the following chapters.

6

Causation

*It isn't mere luck that this morning immediately after I entered
the kitchen the light went on, that when I sat at the breakfast
table, tired and thirsty, hot coffee ran down my throat... These
things accorded to my wishes because part of what happened
were* actions *of mine that causally influenced the world... They*
[actions based on wishes] *make it possible for us to influence
the world instead of being condemned, flowerlike, to take things
as they come.*

> Ralf Stoeker in Walter and Heckmann (Eds.)
> (2003, page 296)

One of the most intractable problems of consciousness is that of
mental causation. How do my *feelings* of thirst and tiredness and
my resulting train of *thought* and *imagination* lead to the *physical
behavior of matter*: I engage in the physical acts of making myself
a cup of coffee and drinking it.

In this chapter I hope to show how idealist panpsychism
gives a lucid, rational solution to the problem of mental
causation. First we need to state the problem, and highlight the
difficulties it causes for physicalists. Recall from Chapter 4 that
physicalism (or *materialism*) is, roughly speaking, the
metaphysical proposal that, at the most fundamental level, the
universe is comprised of material entities, and that these entities
can be characterized completely by their interaction with one
another in accordance with the mathematical laws of
(completed) physics. In particular, the ultimate constituents of
the universe, such as electrons, are not sentient. Physicalism is
motivated by the outstanding success of science, but, as we saw,

it is highly problematic as a philosophy. We will consider first of all how successfully or otherwise physicalists can give an account of mental causation. In doing this we will lay aside the problem, discussed in Chapter 4, of comprehending what physicalists mean when they talk of unobserved physical existence.

The problem of mental causation

Figure 6.1 illustrates the problem of mental causation, and three failed attempts to solve it. I have adopted the convention that supposed actually existing entities (in Figure 6.1 physical states **P**) are shown in bold. Horizontal solid arrows are arrows of causation through time. Dotted arrows show causal links that are disputed, or show merely apparent causation. These conventions have been followed for all the figures in this chapter.

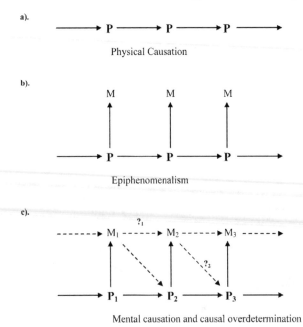

a).

P ⟶ **P** ⟶ **P**

Physical Causation

b).

M   M   M

P ⟶ **P** ⟶ **P**

Epiphenomenalism

c).

M_1 ⟶ M_2 ⟶ M_3

$?_1$ $?_2$

P₁ ⟶ **P₂** ⟶ **P₃**

Mental causation and causal overdetermination

Figure 6.1: The problem of mental causation

In Figure 6.1(a) we see a crude sketch of the physical state **P** of the world as time progresses from left to right. According to physicalists, the physical world is *causally closed* in the sense that its physical state at any one moment is sufficient to determine its state at the next moment (apart from some irreducible randomness).

Because of this causal completeness, there does not seem to be any room for mental causation. One horn of the dilemma is to accept this as a fact, and treat mind as an *epiphenomenon*, without any causal effects whatsoever. Figure 6.1(b) illustrates epiphenomenalism. Physical states fully determine subsequent physical states as before. In certain regions of space (in particular within human brains) physical states **P** give rise to mental states M, but these mental states have no effects whatsoever. The "giving rise to" relationship is symbolized by the upwards-pointing arrows. Thomas Huxley was an epiphenomenalist, but this view has fatal problems:

- My hopes and desires have no effect on the physical world. My wanting coffee cannot cause me to begin to make it. The fact that I do this has an entirely physical cause, namely my previous brain state.
- I cannot engage in a chain of reasoning or form an independent judgment. What appears to be a chain of reasoning or a judgment is merely a reflection of underlying brain states.
- I cannot know that other people's minds exist because their thoughts have no effect whatsoever on their behavior. You are in the same situation. This book gives you no evidence as to what I actually believe about consciousness, nor evidence that I have any thoughts whatsoever. Written or spoken language cannot even be *about* consciousness at all.
- Worst of all I cannot even know that my own mind existed prior to this present moment, because my prior mental life

has no effect either directly or indirectly on my current mental state.

- How is science possible when I as a thinking being have no possibility of interacting with the cosmos? I cannot carry out experiments based upon my ideas because my ideas cannot be translated into physical acts.
- Why do only some physical states give rise to mental states? No one knows what characteristics a physical state must have in order to have an associated mental state.

In all but the last of the above objections, I have regarded myself as being essentially a mind: as being one or more of the instances of M in Figure 6.1(b). Daniel Dennett (1991) regards himself as a strictly physical system, **P**, and he has a different, but equally fatal, objection to epiphenomenalism:

- Regarding myself as a strictly physical system **P**, I have no reason for "believing" (in Dennett's mechanistic, non experiential, non-qualitative sense of the word) in mental states M, because there is no causal path from M to **P** in Figure 6.1(b).

The above problems would be resolved if mental states were somehow *identical* with physical states. In this case, for example, a particular taste of coffee *would just be* a particular pattern of neural firing within my brain. Identity theories are popular, but they have their own problems. They tend to be eliminativist in tenor, especially if one assumes that, once the identity is made, we need no longer speak about tastes of coffee, but can instead substitute talk of neural firings. The major problem for the physicalist who is also a qualia realist is that the identity is obscure given the contrasting characteristics of tastes of coffee and patterns of neural firings. How could such an identity possibly hold? Surely this is something in itself calling out for an explanation. Most identity theorists do not attempt to answer this question, but are content to assert that it must hold, despite its obscurity, because neural events and mental events are well correlated.

The theory to be presented here turns out to be an identity theory, but one with the distinct advantage that the manner in which the identity holds can be lucidly and rationally explained.

Figure 6.1(c) illustrates the other horn of the dilemma. Because of the intractable problems of epiphenomenalism (and of physicalist identity theories) we assume that mind-mind causation exists so that I can engage in chains of reasoning and remember my past mental states, as illustrated by the arrow $?_1$. We also assume that mind-body causation exists, so that I can perform physical tasks at will such as making the coffee. This is illustrated by the arrow $?_2$.

This does not solve the problem, however. The transition from M_1 to M_2 is fully determined by the physical link from P_1 to P_2, together with the upward ("mind arising") links P_1 to M_1 and P_2 to M_2. Under the assumption of the causal completeness of the physical world, the "chain of thought" link $?_1$ is redundant, because state M_2 would have followed from M_1 anyway. Similarly the mind-body link $?_2$ is redundant because P_3 would follow directly from P_2 even in the absence of this link.

Some philosophers have tried to overcome this problem of *causal overdetermination* by making an analogy with situations like a man being shot dead simultaneously by two bullets. Such arguments have never been convincing. A thorough discussion of these problems is given in *Physicalism and Mental Causation*, edited by Sven Walter and Heinz-Dieter Heckmann (2003).

Causal relationships among the classical, hard sciences

The problem of causal overdetermination seems to arise because of the closed loops (squares and triangles) in Figure 6.1(c). It occurred to me that similar closed loops exist in the causal diagrams that describe the hard sciences and their relationships to one another during the period of history when classical physics reigned. These latter closed loops, however, do not give rise to problems of causal overdetermination. Examining such a diagram might therefore provide a clue that would help solve the problem of mental causation.

Figure 6.2 shows a diagram of such causal relationships. By classical science I mean science that is deterministic and does not involve the peculiarities of quantum theory. By hard sciences I mean sciences that deal solely with behavior, and specifically exclude the mind. The soft science of psychology is for example excluded.

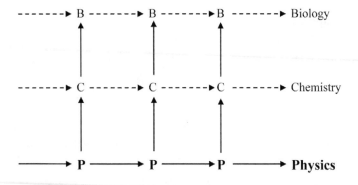

Figure 6.2: Reductionism and causation in the classical physics era

In Figure 6.2, at the bottom level, there is physical causation as before, and once again we assume that the physical level is causally complete. Above physics, the hard sciences are stacked in a natural hierarchy. We might have inserted extra levels, for example placing cellular biology and organic chemistry between biology and chemistry.

At each level there is causality specific to the appropriate discipline. Chemical reactions have causal explanations within the level of chemistry for instance. There are also explanations between these disciplines, but these always proceed from the bottom up. A cat stretches forward with its paw. This is caused by the firing of motor nerve cells causing certain muscle cells to contract. These events in turn have a complicated explanation in terms of chemistry. This chemistry in turn has an explanation in terms of physics. At the level of physics the story ends because physics is the foundational level of science.

At each level, we have an explanation in terms of causation that belongs to that level, and this explanation is true. There are valid explanations of physical events in terms of physical causation, valid explanations of chemical reactions in terms of molecules and ions, and so on. How can each of these levels of explanation be valid, despite there being no suggestion of causal overdetermination? (No one has ever worried about causal overdetermination here.)

The answer is that each higher level science is (at least in principle) no more than a re-description of the science below it in simpler terms. Every statement in chemistry is really no more than a synopsis of a much more complex statement from within the discipline of physics. Each statement in biology could be reduced to a very complicated statement within chemistry. A cat is nothing more than a system of chemicals with a complex specification for putting them together in a catlike manner. The specification is flexible enough to arrive at any cat. We do not care if the cat is black or tabby, and we arrive at the concept of "cat" by throwing away irrelevant information, such as that which gives a cat's pigmentation. The complete specification of a particular cat in terms of chemistry completely fixes its speci-fication in terms of biology. The upward pointing arrows in Figure 6.2 symbolize this throwing away of irrelevant infor-mation.

Within the scheme of Figure 6.2 we say that biology reduces to chemistry, and chemistry reduces to physics. This is the concept of *reductionism,* and I believe it is a useful and powerful one. In this *reductive* scheme causality at each level is likewise no more than a much simplified re-description of causality that is going on at the level below. There is no causal overdetermination. There is only a single fundamental causality at the level of physics that is re-described in ever broader terms. The causal arrows for biology and chemistry are shown dotted for this reason. We can take as an example the metaphor already mentioned of the man who was shot. Here, it is as if he was killed by a slug of metal and by a fast moving collection of elementary particles. He was not shot twice; it is just that the same bullet is described in two different ways.

It is tempting to regard mind as an extra level above that of biology. After all, the mainstream view is that mind only occurs in certain complex biological systems. This move fails for two reasons: First, it implies either the denial or the radical emergence of qualia, and these proposals have been decisively rejected, in Chapter 2 on consciousness and Chapter 4 on existence respectively. Second, we still run into all of the problems of Figure 6.1, but merely set at a higher level. Some people try to avoid these latter problems by evoking a controversial doctrine called *downward causation.* I will not discuss downward causation here, as the first reason given in this paragraph is already decisively fatal.

Present day and 'completed' physics

The twentieth century was dominated by the quantum revolution in physics. Figure 6.3 shows the current situation of physics, with quantum physics sitting below chemistry. There is a question mark about quantum physics, for the reasons already sketched at the end of Chapter 3 on science. Quantum physics is unimpeachable as a theory of human knowledge in that it makes extremely accurate predictions about the results of measurements. The *Copenhagen interpretation* is the popular name for this epistemological understanding of the theory. Rival interpretations of quantum mechanics have attempted to provide an ontology (a theory telling us what exists in the universe), but none have been widely accepted. Figure 6.3 symbolizes this ontological lack, by having no bold nodes representing actual entities, and no solid horizontal arrows representing actual causation.

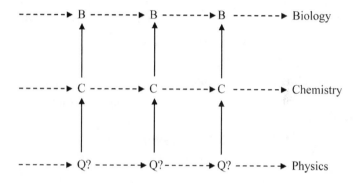

Figure 6.3: Reductionism and causation in the quantum era

The problem is that we need an ontology. We need to know what dinosaurs and cats and water are in and of themselves. For instance, let us try to give a reductive account of water. We know that water is H_2O, and that hydrogen and oxygen are comprised of fundamental particles. (The fundamental entities of nature may instead turn out to have the character of strings or membranes rather than of particles. We are ignoring this unimportant complication.) But we only know these fundamental particles in the context where they are observed and measured by us. Water and fundamental particles had to be around in the universe long before our arrival on the scene, because without their prior existence we could not have evolved. But what is it for a fundamental particle to exist of itself (and not in the context of being measured)? We need an ontology for fundamental particles. Without it, Figure 6.3 is like a castle built on air, and reductionism fails.

This argument strongly suggests that there has to be an ontological level below the level of present-day or even completed physics. Figure 6.4 sketches how a completed (or at least more complete) physics might look. Below the level of chemistry there is the Copenhagen Quantum epistemology (CQ): essentially this is just present-day quantum mechanics, but the name emphasizes the correct Copenhagen understanding of the theory as being one of epistemology. The epistemological character of quantum mechanics, to which all of the hard sciences reduce, validates the point made in Chapter 4 that the whole of the hard sciences are about collating and predicting human experiences of the appearances of the world.

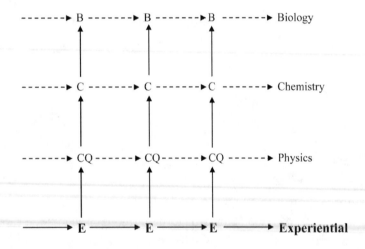

Figure 6.4: Reductionism and causation according to idealist panpsychism

The bottom layer of Figure 6.4 is the *experiential layer* which contains the fundamental particles as they are in and of themselves. Causation happens at this fundamental ontological layer because all causation is between actually existing objects, and not merely between appearances. The layer is depicted in bold because of these ontological claims. There are very good reasons from the character of quantum theory (from the Heisenberg indeterminacy principle amongst other things) for supposing that the ontological layer will be forever beyond the reach of experimental observation, although we might still hope to model it mathematically.

I will call the type of reductionism featured in Figure 6.4 *rabbit-hole reductionism*. As with conventional reductionism, descriptions in the various hard sciences all reduce to description at the level of (completed) physics. However, I am insisting that the hard sciences can provide nothing more than mathematical descriptions of appearances. With completed physics the description is mathematically unsurpassable, in that no observation or experiment could contradict it, but it remains no more than a description of appearances. There is one final stage of reduction "down the rabbit hole", from the perfectly delineated appearances of completed physics, to the actualities beneath.

Causation and idealist panpsychism

The **thesis** I wish to propose is that: *the fundamental entities of the ontological layer (which present themselves to physicists as particles, strings, membranes, or whatever) are in actuality the fundamental experiential entities discussed in the previous chapter on idealist panpsychism.*

Idealist panpsychism is a variety of identity theory, but it is unique in that it clearly explains how the things being identified can have different properties. The explanation boils down to the fact that an object and its appearance to others can have different properties. The object and its appearance both refer to one identical thing: the object itself. An electron, for example, is in fact an experiential entity. This is what the electron *really is*. More sophisticated experiential entities (physicists) observe the electron. These observations constitute how the electron appears to the physicists. The electron-as-it-is-in-itself and the electron-as-it-appears-to-physicists refer to one and only one entity, namely the electron-as-it-is-in-itself – a particular type of ultimate experiential entity.

In Figure 6.4, a particular node **E** might represent an electron-as-it-is-in-itself, and the node CQ above it represents this same electron, but as-it-appears-to-physicists.

Thesis: *All (actual) causality in idealist panpsychism is between experiential entities, which can act upon each other with a degree of spontaneity according to their percepts.*

This is because genuine causality can only take place between things that actually exist. There can only be apparent causation between what are merely the appearances of things. As we have stated many times, physics does no more than to describe systematically the appearance of actualities. So, the probabilistic behavior of fundamental particles, described by physics, is no more than a reflection of this underlying actual causality, which is experiential in character.

Experiential entities are supposed to exist in hierarchies, and the experiential state of beings at a higher level is in part determined by the states of beings at the next lower level. For example, the perceptual state of an atom depends in large part upon the perceptual states of the elementary particles that comprise it. Similarly the perceptual state of a cell depends in part on the perceptual states of the molecules that comprise it. This allows for the possibility of more complex perceptual structures to be built up in higher levels of the hierarchy.

Questions and answers about causation

Q: Isn't this highly implausible? In order to explain consciousness you propose that it resides in an ontological layer below the level of science and forever beyond measurement.

A: Some extra layer is needed anyway, to provide an ontology for the theory of evolution for instance. (We saw in Chapter 4 that physicalists could give no satisfactory definition of material existence.) It sits below the lowest level of physics with upward pointing arrows to symbolize the fact that reality causes appearance.

Q: If this ontological layer is beyond the level of measurement, how are we to envisage it?

A: An electron, say, is a primitive experiential entity, which is continually in holistic, perceptual encounter with all the other entities in its vicinity. Some of these other entities may occasionally constitute experimental probes by a scientist. The electron will not be entirely characterized by experimental probes for three reasons: First, the electron invariably perceives other entities in its vicinity besides the scientist's probing, and these are at least partly hidden from the scientist. Second, the principle of indeterminacy in quantum mechanics means that if, say, the electron's exact position is measured, then its momentum is completely indeterminate, and vice versa. Finally, the electron is a volitional entity, and is an active participant in the cosmos. Even if the scientist could magically be given a complete mathematical description of the electron's ontological or perceptual state E (and recall that this state is not part of even completed physics), this would still not be enough to determine its future.

Q: How will we know about experiential entities if they are forever beyond the reach of measurement?

A: Although they are beyond measurement, perhaps we can guess a mathematical model for the percepts of ultimate experiential entities (the elementary particles of physics), and also model how these percepts combine as the particles combine. This, in principle, could give a mathematical structure to percepts within the human brain that could be compared with verbal reports. In practice this would be incredibly difficult, but at least it shows that consciousness is not a mystery that we have no conceptual grip on.

Q: How can there be any causality below the level of the physical world? I thought you claimed that the physical world must be causally closed.

A: I said that physicalists took this view. However, my own belief is that there is no causation at the level of physics, and there is no rational argument to prove such causal closure. This is in line with the opinion of philosopher David Hume who famously asserted that, on the basis of observation alone, we can prove nothing definite about causation; we can only talk of correlations among appearances. The belief that the physical world must be causally closed probably arises from the overconfidence of physicalists that they have an intuitive grasp of the essence of matter.

(Hume, adopting a skeptical position, denied that there was any such thing as causation; physicalists assume that causation exists at the level of physics; I am proposing that causality exists at the experiential level. These are three distinct metaphysical hypotheses and may be compared with one another by contrasting the overall scope and explanatory power of the metaphysical systems of which they are part.)

Q: How can you be sure that causality truly resides in this ontological layer?

A: The ontological layer is by definition the layer where the ultimate realities of the universe lie. Real causality must be between real entities. John Searle puts it this way in his very different analysis of causation, (1984, pages 64-5, (emphasis added)), "The form of causation that we are discussing here is quite different from the standard form of causation as described in philosophical textbooks. It is not a matter of regularities or covering laws or constant conjunctions. In fact I think it's much closer to our commonsense notion of causation, where we just mean that *something makes something else happen...*"

Q: Why isn't there causation at the bottom level of physics? Shouldn't there be solid horizontal arrows connecting CQ and

CQ in Figure 6.4?

A: No. Even completed physics just deals with the mathematical structure of appearance, and the appearance of causation. Experiential entities and their interactions are the underlying realities that cause these appearances. In Plato's allegory of the cave, it would be false to assert that the shadow of the bat *actually caused* the change in direction of the shadow of the ball. Rather, a bat causes a change of direction in a ball, and their shadows mimic this fact.

Q: Why place experiential entities in the ontological layer?

A: The previous two chapters have already explained that doing this clarifies the concepts of what it is for the universe, and the objects within it, actually to exist. This chapter has shown how it helps to solve, at least in principle, the problem of mental causation.

Q: How does Figure 6.4 explain mind-mind causation (as in a train of thought)?

A: The human brain comprises a hierarchical group of experiential entities. These experiential entities have causal effects on each other throughout the course of time. This causation is depicted in the horizontal arrows from **E** to **E** across the base of Figure 6.4.

Q: And mind-body causation?

A: Imagine a group of scientists observing a living human brain. This brain is in truth a system of experiential entities. As these entities interact over time, this is reflected in the changing appearances that the system presents in the minds of the onlookers.

(As I have argued in Chapter 4, these changing appearances are precisely the brain's developing empirical state. In contrast to physicalists, the claim that I am making here is that there is more to a brain – or to any entity – than the totality of what may be discovered by empirical methods.)

Motor neurons, as experiential systems, can equally perceive aspects of the brain's empirical state and moreover act on such percepts. As a result they can fire causing muscles to contract.

Q: How do you explain body-mind causation?

A: It is just a basic fact about experiential entities that they have percepts of other experiential entities, and furthermore they perceive them as objects (or bodies). We are assuming that experiential entities can alter their behavior according to their percepts, and so we have body-mind causation.

Q: Isn't this talk of hierarchies of experiential entities a little vague?

A: Yes, I admit this. I am relying heavily on the fact that the theory presented here is an identity theory, and that it is not implausible that hierarchies of experiential entities reflect the hierarchies of structures that are met with in physics, biology and the other sciences. Gregg Rosenberg (2004) has a more highly developed theory of hierarchies within panpsychism.

Q: The spontaneity that experiential entities possess, which is based on their percepts, must be identical to the randomness witnessed in elementary particles. Isn't this just empty metaphysics – a mere comforting use of language? How, for example, can such spontaneity be used to construct a worthwhile theory of free will?

A: The theory presented here does have real content and physical consequences. It implies that fundamental empirical facts of physics are essential for consciousness. In particular, quantum effects are essential to the functioning of the brain, and so no device in which neurons were replaced by silicon chips that acted like classical computers would be sufficient for consciousness. Subsequent chapters will explore this quantum nature and present a theory of fee will.

7

Résumé

Our ship floats becalmed, and the captain, having made us scrub, polish and mend everything possible on board, has finally allowed us some time on deck. To the huffing tune of a concertina and the clacking of dominoes, there is a chance for us crewmates to review the log of our quest.

-oOo-

The last three chapters have argued for idealist panpsychism: the thesis that the fundamental level of reality sits below the level of physics, and is comprised entirely of experiential entities that can organize themselves into hierarchies. There is nothing else to the universe apart from such entities, which are in essence minds. This chapter gives a brief résumé of these arguments.

Résumé

In **Chapter 4** we wanted to capture formally the intuitive notion of what it was for an object such as a rock or a person *actually* or *concretely to exist* in our universe. We considered four concepts of existence, starting from the most direct and familiar, and ending with the most abstract.

First, there is our own *experiential existence* as minds. If we are not in the grip of philosophical doubt, we are confident of the existence of other minds.

Second, we considered the *empirical existence* of objects in the world that can be inferred by collating the experiences of several minds. Such objects include the Moon, mountains, rocks, lakes, trees, worms, elephants, ice cream and baked beans. All of these things can be seen, and some can also be felt and tasted.

We also allowed for the empirical existence of other entities that we cannot experience directly, but whose existence explains (by means of a particular theory) certain facts of our experience. Atoms come under this subheading, for example, because atomic theory explains, among many other things, why we see chemicals reacting in certain fixed proportions. Magnetic fields revealed by iron filings give another example.

We have no access to the external world except through our percepts. Moreover, we have no way of distinguishing between reality and illusion except by seeking confirmation from other minds. These are two reasons why the existence of mind precedes empirical existence in certainty and directness. These facts also remove the sting from the philosophical problem of "other minds". If we are confident of the existence of such objects as are listed above, then we should have no rational doubts about the existence of other minds, because the concept of empirical existence depends upon the existence of other minds.

An interesting class of physical objects is that of our own bodies. We can associate each of our minds with its own particular body. However, in the spirit of the previous paragraph, even our own bodies are unknown to us except as a structure of appearances that can reliably be shared and collated by ourselves and other minds.

Third is the concept of material existence. According to the dominant materialist or physicalist paradigm, mind did not arise in our universe until after the advent of life. If this assumption is correct, we need a concept describing the existence of things in the world in the absence of mind. This led to attempts to define another concept: the *material existence* of material objects obeying the mathematical laws of physics, without regard to observation by experiential beings. The chapter went to great lengths to show that no satisfactory definition of material existence could be given, as, in the absence of experiential beings, material existence invariably collapsed into mere *mathematical existence* (our fourth type of existence).

Some concept of material existence is essential if physicalism is true. If an adequate definition cannot be given then this is strong evidence that physicalism is false. Moreover, the chapter provided (I believe powerful) arguments that the initial emergence of consciousness, essential for physicalism, is impossible. The arguments were lengthy but were based on the idea that, since material existence is indistinguishable from mathematical existence, any proof of the emergence of consciousness in the early universe can be translated into the proof of the emergence of qualitative experiences from an abstract mathematical system, and this is absurd.

Over the course of the chapter I showed that the human discipline of physics, as it is in fact practiced, takes as its raw data particular regular structures within our experiences. Physicists single out those structures that can reliably be shared with others and collated, and takes them to be veridical in the sense that certain spatiotemporal entities are postulated, which exist and give rise to these experiences. The discipline of physics can tell us nothing about these spatiotemporal entities save for their formal mathematical relationships between one another, and that they in some unexplained way give rise to our experiences. Of itself, moreover, physics can tell us nothing about either space or time beyond formal mathematical structure.

Chapter 4 concluded by abandoning physicalism and adopting panpsychism. I made the strong metaphysical claim that to *actually* or *concretely exist* in our world, and in all possible worlds, just *is* to be an experiential entity, or a system of experiential entities, where an *experiential entity* has both experiential existence and empirical existence inseparably conjoined. An experiential entity is, in its essence, a mind, but it also has the property that other such entities can perceive it. The "body" of an experiential entity is not composed of any extra substance or stuff. The "existence of its physical body" amounts to *no more than the empirical fact that this entity or mind can be observed by others* in some systematic, intersubjective way.

Chapter 5 on idealist panpsychism continues the argument. Panpsychism is the assertion that experiential entities are fundamental to and omnipresent throughout the cosmos, both in space and in time. There is nothing absurd or self-contradictory about panpsychism, despite the claims of some philosophers, and we should adopt it as the most straightforward hypothesis. Indeed, any attempt to avoid panpsychism founders irredeemably on the rock of emergence as we have already learned.

There was an interlude in which I described and critiqued Max Tegmark's unusual and strongly reductionist position, in which we and our universe are nothing other than a highly complex, formal mathematical object (2003). In contrast to this, I gave an elementary example of a dodecahedral universe, illustrating how mind and body might in principle be connected according to idealist panpsychism. The model illustrated: how mind is invisible to physics (is private); how mind is subjective (is perspectival); how mind has only partial information about the surrounding universe; and how physics can be constructed by combining the percepts of observers.

I have used the term *idealist* panpsychism, because everything that exists is in essence a mind, or is composed of minds. Most forms of idealism have been criticized on the grounds that they deny the reality of the objects that give rise to our experiences. The same accusation cannot be leveled at idealist panpsychism. Idealist panpsychism asserts that the Moon really does exist. It exists concretely as a hierarchy of experiential entities in a community of mutual observation and interaction. The Moon is much simpler than a human community, but the existence of the Moon, which is in truth a system of experiential entities, has its analogue in the existence of a human community. Thus, contrary to common expectation, idealist panpsychism gives a much clearer account of the reality of the Moon than does physicalism. According to idealist panpsychism, the Moon is now, and has always been, just as concrete a thing as a toothache, or as real as our verifiable experiences while having coffee with friends.

Physicalism gives no coherent account of what matter is in and of itself. For example, according to physicalists, when the Moon is behind clouds what is it beyond a mere abstraction, made out of abstractions? The same applies to the Moon as it was five billion years ago. (As we have seen, the claim that matter is spatiotemporal merely leads to more abstractions.) Physicalists might affirm that what distinguishes the Moon – or any broadly similar clump of insentient matter such as a piece of slime – from an abstraction is its potential for causing qualitative human experiences. However, if one accepts that this potential is the *sole* concrete property possessed by such insentient clumps, then explaining how primitive qualitative experiences initially came into being is obviously impossible. Moreover, no physicalist has ever proposed any additional concrete property or fact about any of the matter that existed in the very early universe – because it is the crux of their position to deny that any such additional facts exist.

Russell, Eddington, Chalmers and others, following in the footsteps of Leibniz (1714) take the noumenon (reality) behind the phenomenon (appearance) of an object to be mentalistic in character. In the words of David Chalmers, "There is only one class of intrinsic, nonrelational property with which we have any direct familiarity, and this is the class of phenomenal properties... Perhaps, as Russell suggested, at least some of the intrinsic properties of the physical are themselves a variety of phenomenal property?" (1996, pages 153-4). Idealist panpsychism goes somewhat further and takes the fundamental particles and other entities of physics to be extremely primitive but fully-fledged experiential entities. The theory thus gives a clear answer as to what matter is, by asserting that matter exists in the same way that we do ourselves.

Chapter 6 on causation showed by means of diagrams that experiential entities are best regarded as lying at a level below that of (even completed) physics. This results in a comprehensible account, wherein all causation is actually (lawful, mental) causation among these experiential entities, and this gives rise to apparent causation at the level of physics. In other words, mind-mind causation (as fundamental) gives rise to the appearance of body-body causation, describable in terms of the laws of physics. It is thus not valid to assert, as physicalists do, that the physical world is causally closed: rather, there is only lawful regularity at this level. This chapter also explains mind-body and body-mind causation.

By analogy with physics-as-a-human-discipline, already discussed, idealist panpsychism goes on to define the (true and thus completed) physics-of-the-world in empirical terms, as a secondary characteristic of the universe, which is arrived at by collating the experiences of *all* experiential entities. (This is in contrast to physicalism which takes the physics-of-the-world as being primary, foundational and not-wholly-empirical.)

Idealist panpsychism is a variety of identity theory, but it is unique in that it straightforwardly explains how the two things being identified can have different properties. The explanation boils down to the commonplace fact that an object and the appearance that it presents to others can have different properties. The object and its appearance both refer to one identical thing: the object itself. For instance, I might point to a dark shape silhouetted by the Sun and exclaim, "There's Jim!" In idealist panpsychism an electron, for example, is in fact an experiential entity or mind. This is what the electron *really and truly is* in itself. More sophisticated experiential entities (physicists) observe the electron. These observations constitute how the electron appears to the physicists. Despite their different characteristics, the electron-as-it-is-in-itself and the electron-as-it-appears-to-physicists refer to one and only one entity, namely the electron-as-it-is-in-itself – a particular, elementary type of experiential entity.

As yet, the claim that experiential entities can form themselves into hierarchies has not been substantiated. In this book I will do just a little to show how this claim might be satisfied, at least in principle, by going on to examine some of the nascent quantum approaches to mind.

-oOo-

The gentle, midnight ocean sparkles with phosphorescence, imitating the stars, so that our ship seems becalmed in space.

Roger, the sharp-eyed lookout of the motley crew, spies a little mermaid, playing off the port bow. She reclines half out of the water, modestly combing her auburn hair, while her lower half flashes as a fish's tail. It is a quantum tail, and, underneath the ripples, it breaks up into many shimmering copies, before repeatedly re-forming itself.

She is a sign of good fortune and, at this moment, a breeze stirs life into the limp sails causing the rigging to creak. The white plume of a bow wave appears, and we sail into the quantum world.

8

Quantum Mind

I don't know any better illustration of [quantum behavior] *than the famous picture by Charles Adams of the skier who comes to a tree with his pair of skis and then one sees the skier after he's passed. One track has gone on the left-hand side of the tree and the second track has gone on the right-hand side, but you don't see any revelation of how the skier has completed this miracle!*

John A. Wheeler, in Davies and Brown (1986, page 65)

Previous chapters have argued for idealist panpsychism: the thesis that the fundamental level of reality sits below the level of even completed physics, and consists entirely of experiential entities that can organize themselves into hierarchical systems. Even a fully completed physics could not deal directly with the ultimate constituents of reality. Rather, it could deal only with the structure of the appearances of these constituents, which are in essence minds. The last chapter gave a résumé of these arguments.

This chapter asks: what do we expect the properties and characteristics of completed physics to be if these arguments are true? It then goes on to describe in general terms quantum physics, the closest approach we have to completed, fundamental physics at the present epoch, and shows that this has the properties and characteristics as predicted under the hypothesis of idealist panpsychism.

The direction of the argument goes from idealist panpsychism towards predicting the bizarre properties of quantum physics. It does not go in the opposite direction, first describing quantum physics, and then arguing from this description that the fundamental units of reality must be experiential entities. Arguing in this latter direction would be unconvincing because there is controversy as to what quantum theory means in terms of reality, with many conflicting interpretations being offered.

The chapter concludes by suggesting some points of connection between quantum mechanics and idealist panpsychism.

Quantum approaches to mind

A significant minority of philosophers and scientists have taken quantum physics to be a key concept in attempting to solve the mind-body problem. Among those taking this approach are David Bohm in his book *Wholeness and the Implicate Order* (1980) and also in *The Undivided Universe* (1993), written in conjunction with Basil Hiley; Roger Penrose with his books *The Emperor's New Mind* (1989) and *Shadows of the Mind* (1995), (the latter influenced by his collaborator Stuart Hameroff); David Hodgson in *The Mind Matters* (1991); William Seager in *Theories of Consciousness* (1999); and Henry Stapp in *Mind, Matter and Quantum Mechanics* (2004). This minority has been sufficiently large to support a series of conferences dedicated to this approach. The first, *Quantum Mind 1999*, took place in Flagstaff, Arizona. *Quantum Mind 2003* was held in Tucson, Arizona, and *Quantum Mind 2007* in Salzburg, Austria. I was lucky enough to attend and give short talks at these latter two conferences even though I am not an academic. The 2003 conference was just a few months after Ana María's death, and gave me a much-needed distraction.

Not all theories of quantum mind are panpsychist in character, but many are. Once you have affirmed that mind is associated with quantum, it is at least possible that mind in some diluted form is omnipresent throughout the universe.

Predictions of idealist panpsychism

Idealist panpsychism makes six predictions about the properties and characteristics of fundamental physics. The first four apply to panpsychism in general:

1. *The behavior of an elementary entity depends upon the detailed configuration of all of the other entities in its environment*

This is because panpsychism treats the fundamental units of nature as being experiential in character. They can perceive their environment, and act according to the whole of this percept.

2. *Fundamental physics is information-theoretical in character*

This is because experiential entities have incomplete percepts of one another, and act on the information or knowledge contained in these percepts.

3. *Elementary entities can amalgamate to form indecomposable compound entities*

We presume that a complex mind such as the human mind is built from successive hierarchies of experiential entities, beginning with fundamental experiential entities that correspond to the ultimates of physics. Let us call the latter *experiential ultimates*. The problem of explaining how these hierarchies are built is called the *combination problem* of panpsychism (Skrbina, 2005, pages 145-149). Human minds have a recognizably coherent psychic unity which, although imperfect, is clearly more unified than it could ever be if the human brain were nothing more than a disorganized heap of independently acting experiential ultimates. Minds must therefore be able to amalgamate into compound minds. This has to take place at all levels, from the level of experiential ultimates to the level of the human brain.

The proposal of point 3 is that the psychic unity of each compound mind (at any level of complexity) manifests itself as indecomposable behavioral unity when this mind is observed as a physical object (or system) by other experiential entities.

4. *Fundamental physics will be found to be inextricably bound up with consciousness*

Panpsychism clearly predicts that this will be the case. Whether or not this is actually true is controversial, as we shall see.

The final two points are specific to idealist panpsychism. (Different theories of panpsychism will have different things to say about ontology and mental causation. Some say little at all.)

5. *Fundamental physics will have difficulties in describing a coherent ontology*

We can ask of a theory: What do the equations tell us about what is real and what is truly happening? Idealist panpsychism is unusual in that it posits that the ontological layer exists *below* the level of physics. The structured percepts that constitute experiential entities are invisible to completed physics, as was seen in the dodecahedral example of Chapter 5. Moreover, even completed physics is no more than the most fundamental level of appearance, as discussed in Chapters 5 and 6. Worldviews that do not recognize these facts will be in difficulty if they try to fix ontology at the level of (current or even completed) physics.

6. *In any given environment, elementary entities show an irreducible spontaneity of behavior*

This last point does not follow from what has so far been

proposed. It is conceivable to have a deterministic version of idealist panpsychism in which the percept of each entity at any given time determines precisely what is going to happen next. However, such determinism is implausible as it contradicts the everyday view we have of ourselves as persons having some limited freedom, able to a certain extent to choose our own goals in life. I have promised to maintain such everyday concepts whenever this can be done without contradiction. Chapter 10 will argue for the coherence of free will.

The character of classical theory

How do classical theories, for example Newtonian mechanics, match up with the above six predictions about the character of fundamental physics?

For points 1 and 2, while it is true that a given atom is instantaneously gravitationally attracted by every other atom in the universe, this attraction falls off rapidly with distance. Moreover, the way that these attractions combine does not provide the given atom much information about the configuration of the others. Points 1 and 2 are thus satisfied, but only in a way that is far too trivial to be consistent with panpsychism.

Regarding point 3, and taking water for example. Water is a composite of two hydrogen atoms with an oxygen atom, but according to classical physics this composition is mere adhesion due to electrical forces. As such, even granting panpsychism, a water molecule cannot be regarded as an indecomposable unity that could be useful as the first stage in building a unified, complex mind. The combination problem is insoluble using classical physics.

Points 4 and 5 are false because classical theories cleanly model the world independently of human observers. In classical theories, elementary particles can be regarded as miniature billiard balls that are fully and clearly characterized by their properties (mass, diameter, charge and so on). Point 6 is false because these theories are deterministic.

Here all six predictions that idealist panpsychism makes about the character of physics fail. The same conclusions would be reached for any classical theory, such as general relativity. If classical theories gave our only description of our universe, then the prospects for idealist panpsychism would be extremely poor, despite the extensive arguments of Chapters 4 through 7.

The character of quantum theory

We need to see whether the fundamental physics of the present day fares any better against the six points made above.

Point 1: *The behavior of an elementary entity depends upon the detailed configuration of all of the other entities in its environment*

This is certainly true. If, for example, a particle is launched into any spatially distributed environment of apparatus and detectors, then the probability that it will arrive at any particular detector depends upon the entire environment (Mattuck, 1992, pages 28-36). Moreover, in popular accounts of this fact some scientists are lead into making use of panpsychist metaphors. In describing Young's double slits experiment, Figure 3.1, Davies and Brown say:

> *Quantum particles do not have well-defined paths in space. It is sometimes convenient to think of each particle as somehow possessing an infinity of different paths, each of which contributes to its behaviour. These threads, or routes, thread through both holes in the screen, and encode information about each. This is how the particle can keep track of what is happening throughout an extended region of space. The fuzziness in its activity enables it to 'feel out' many different routes.*
>
> *Suppose a disbelieving physicist were to station detectors in front of the two holes to ascertain in advance towards which hole a particular electron was heading. Could not the physicist*

then suddenly block the other hole without the electron 'knowing', leaving its motion unaltered? If we analyse the situation, taking into account Heisenberg's uncertainty principle, then we can see that nature outmanoeuvres the wily physicist... Only if we decide not to trace the electron's route will its 'knowledge' of both routes be displayed.

Davies and Brown (1986, pages 8-9)

In the above quotation, Davies and Brown have put the expressions 'feel out', 'knowing' and 'knows' in single quotes to denote that they intend them to be taken metaphorically. An idealist panpsychist would take these expressions almost literally: quantum particles are sentient, but do not have any cognitive powers.

Physicist Richard Feynman, by no means a panpsychist, is lead into making a similar metaphor:

So light doesn't really travel only in a straight line; it 'smells' the neighbouring paths around it.

Feynman (1990, page 54)

Point 2: *Fundamental physics is information-theoretical in character*

This is uncontroversial, and quantum computing and quantum cryptography are currently active areas for research. See for example *The Physics of Quantum Information*, edited by Bouwmeester, Ekert and Zeilinger (2000). Rather than operating with classical *bits* of information (either 0 or 1), proposed quantum computers work with *qubits*, or quantum bits. Each qubit's state can be expressed as a *superposition* that is simultaneously *both 0 and 1* in various combined amounts, and the qubit's state is also *coherent* in the sense that it can undergo interference.

Quantum computers as currently conceived have exactly the same power as conventional computers in the sense that they can answer exactly the same set of problems. The advantage of quantum computers is that, by working with qubits, they have effectively infinite parallelism. They can quickly solve problems that would take a conventional computer longer than the age of the universe to answer. For example, if quantum computers become a reality, then all our banking systems would have to improve their existing methods of encryption, because quantum computers could break these easily.

A major difficulty in the development of quantum computers is that of *decoherence*. Even the tiniest interaction of a qubit with the surrounding environment will destroy its superposed state, leaving only an incoherent mixture of states, still both 0 and 1, but now no longer able to undergo interference, see Bouwmeester, Ekert and Zeilinger (2000, pages 1-4). This has lead to the criticism that quantum mind is a hopeless concept because significant quantum coherent states could not possibly exist in the warm, wet brain. We will see below that physicist Henry Stapp has a well-developed answer to this criticism.

Point 3: *Elementary entities can amalgamate to form indecomposable compound entities*

Quantum theory incontrovertibly substantiates this fact, which has been experimentally tested. The technical term for this indecomposable amalgamation is *entanglement*. In the early days of quantum mechanics, Einstein foresaw consequences of the theory in which widely separated particles could sometimes behave in such a way that their states were inextricably linked, so that measurement of one particle would "instantaneously" change the properties of its partner. He wrote a paper in 1935 along with colleagues Podolsky and Rosen rejecting this "spooky action at a distance," as he called it. In contrast, Niels Bohr replied that this was just the way (our experience of) the world was according to quantum theory, and there the matter rested for thirty years.

In 1965 physicist John Bell investigated the topic. He found a statistical inequality that must be true if Einstein was correct in his assertion that there was no spooky action at a distance. This enabled quantum theory to be put to the test, and in 1982 Alain Aspect and colleagues published one of the most successful experiments proving that in some circumstances elementary particles did indeed break Bell's inequality. This confirmed the spooky fact of entanglement as predicted by quantum theory. *The Ghost in the Atom* edited by Davies and Brown (1986) was published for laypeople as a celebration of Aspect's achievement. It gives an authoritative account of this experiment and the history leading up to it.

Point 4: *Fundamental physics will be found to be inextricably bound up with consciousness*

This is controversial. The dominant, battle tested Copenhagen interpretation of quantum mechanics certainly takes the view that consciousness is essential. In *The Ghost in the Atom* (Davies and Brown, 1986) Rudolph Peierls says that the wave function tells us about our knowledge of a system and that the so-called "collapse of the wave function" occurs when a *conscious* (his emphasis) observer makes an observation (page 73) thus changing the observer's state of knowledge. Peierls emphasizes that the theory is expressed entirely in terms of knowledge and says nothing about "reality", a word whose meaning is unclear in this context. Peierls does not believe that an inanimate object such as a computer or photographic plate could collapse the wave function (page 74). John Wheeler understands the Copenhagen interpretation somewhat differently. He believes that the blackening of a grain of a photographic plate is a real event – an irreversible amplification of a quantum event. However, the information stored on the plate is not *used* until it has been observed by a community of observers (page 63). This concept of used information is closely related to the definition of *empirical existence* given here earlier in Chapter 4.

Nobel laureate Eugene Wigner tried to give an ontology to quantum mechanics by arguing that the first consciousness to observe the system caused the collapse of the wave function as a real physical event. This theory has been much criticized on the grounds that it is not clear what constitutes a conscious system.

Most other interpretations have been devised in an attempt to avoid the role of consciousness at the level of physics. Taking examples again from eminent physicists interviewed for *The Ghost in the Atom*: David Deutsch is associated with the "many universes" interpretation, useful for cosmology (page 91); John Taylor is an advocate of the "statistical interpretation" in which the theory can only be meaningfully applied to ensembles of identically prepared quantum systems (pages 113, 115); and David Bohm proposed a non-local hidden-variable theory (page 119). These attempts to devise alternative interpretations of quantum mechanics all eliminate a causal role for consciousness in the world. This effectively eliminates consciousness itself, even if this is not their proponents' intention. Such alternatives to the Copenhagen interpretation have been criticized by several physicists. See for example Henry Stapp's critique in *Mindful Universe* (2007) Chapter 10.

Point 5: *Fundamental physics will have difficulties in describing a coherent ontology*

This is a plain historical fact about quantum mechanics. The Copenhagen interpretation is unassailable, but only describes an epistemology. Alternative attempts at interpreting quantum mechanics have tried to give an ontology, but all of these are problematic. There is no doubt that if a clear, unproblematic ontology were to be presented then physicists worldwide would vigorously acclaim both it and its authors. This has not yet happened.

Point 6: *In any given environment, elementary entities show an irreducible spontaneity of behavior*

This is an *empirical fact* about quantum mechanics. No matter how tightly we constrain the experimental setup, and no matter how tightly we try to fix the prior quantum state of an elementary entity, the final, observed state of that entity can only ever be determined probabilistically. See, for example, Feynman (1990, page 19).

While it is true that David Bohm's model of quantum theory is deterministic, this determinism is hidden from observers. Bohm himself did not think that his theory was more than a stopgap to deeper understanding (1980, Chapters 4 and 7). In my opinion, the excellent empirical evidence for point 6 carries more weight than Bohm's speculation about an essentially unobservable determinism.

We see that idealist panpsychism successfully predicts all six of these bizarre characteristics of quantum mechanics, whereas physicalism predicts none of them. Contrary to what some critics assert, elementary entities do give some signs of possessing experience.

The parable of the plate

A put-down is quite frequently directed at advocates of quantum approaches to mind. Richard Grush and Patricia Churchland attribute it to Itamar Pitowski and put it thus:

> *(1) We really do not understand the nature of consciousness; (2) the only things in the physical world we really do not understand are quantum-level phenomena; (3) therefore these are probably the same mystery.*
>
> Grush and Churchland (1995, page 11)

This is a false accusation. The advocates of quantum mind do more than express an invalid 3-point syllogism. Everyone in the field attempts to develop an explicit theory to explain the connection between properties of consciousness and quantum properties. The accusation avoids coming to grips with the specifics of each such theory. Moreover, by presenting such a caricature, these accusers turn attention away from the glaring paradoxes of all physicalist explanations.

I wish to use a parable to show that, on the contrary, attempting to relate these two great mysteries is a sensible procedure:

> *Imagine that you have found two pieces of pottery in a field. Each piece seems to be half of a plate, and each has a broken edge. What is the sensible procedure in this situation? Clearly it is to place the broken edges together to see if the pieces make a single plate. If they do not match, one can immediately conclude that either there is a third piece plate which belongs between them, or alternatively that the two pieces come from different plates. In either case of failure to match, the logical next step is to look for additional pieces of pottery. It would be foolish to try to match the broken edge of one piece of plate with the unbroken part of the circumference of the other.*

So many approaches to consciousness emulate the latter "foolish" procedure. The method of most neuroscientists is to try to explain brain function and simultaneously to try to find what is called the "neural correlate of consciousness". Christof Koch believes that as neuroscience advances the mind-body problem will "dissolve." The fallacy is that the more successful neuroscience is, and the more the function of the brain is explained, then the more it becomes analogous to the unbroken edge of the plate. If neuroscience were ever to explain fully (in behavioral terms) the functioning of a particular portion of the brain that is associated with a particular conscious state, then that conscious state could only be a useless, epiphenomenal appendage. As neuroscience progresses in explaining brain behavior in physical, functional terms, the problem of consciousness becomes more mysterious not less.

The work of neuroscientists is of the utmost value in understanding brain function, and finding the neural correlates of consciousness will be a major step towards solving the mind-body problem. It only becomes "foolish" if one believes that even a completed neuroscience and a perfect list of neural correlates will, of themselves, have solved the hard problem. There still remains David Chalmers' question, "Why does this brain state have to *feel* like this?"

Advocates of strong AI are following a truly foolish procedure. To say that a robot is conscious is like gluing a broken piece of plate to one that is already whole. We are already certain that with a computer-controlled robot we have a complete, classical, functional explanation for its behavior. We can conclude that robots are certainly not conscious in any significant sense. For a robot to have a consciousness comparable to our own would be for it to possess a useless, epiphenomenal appendage.

According to idealist panpsychists there must be some miniscule consciousness associated with any computer or robot, but this consciousness would not be anything like ours. A computer successfully imitating a human (by passing the Turing Test) would have essentially the same trivial degree of low-level consciousness as a computer running a word-processing program, or one that is just on standby.

Quantum mind and the parable of the plate

What happens if we follow the advice of the parable of the plate and try to place the two great mysteries of quantum mechanics and the mind-body problem together? Do the jagged edges fit?

A tremendous fit is this: **The mind-body problem arises from an excess of ontology.** There are extra ingredients to the world, notably qualia, and the possessors of those qualia. These extra ingredients certainly cannot be fitted into classical physics. **The mystery of quantum mechanics consists in its lack of an ontology.** As we have seen, the Copenhagen School describes an unimpeachable epistemology. It is a matter of historical fact that the theory lacks an agreed ontology.

Earlier in the chapter I described six predictions about the character of fundamental physics arising from idealist panpsychism, all of these predictions held, and there are no consequences of idealist panpsychism that contradict physics. The first four predictions apply to many forms of panpsychism. The fifth point is specific to idealist panpsychism and gives an explanation for the above tremendous fit. The case for idealist panpsychism is thus worthy of serious attention, despite its counterintuitive character.

Idealist panpsychism and quantum mechanics
We are now ready to suggest some points of connection between idealist panpsychism and quantum mechanics. These suggestions can be no more than preliminary and tentative.

1. The Heisenberg ontology
The case was made in Chapter 3 that the universe must have some fundamental ontology. We therefore need to relate quantum mechanics to some ontology, even if this can only be sketched provisionally and incompletely. Throughout *Mind, Matter and Quantum Mechanics* (2004) Henry Stapp describes the ontology favored by Werner Heisenberg. In it, the wave function of the universe is real and concrete, and is interpreted as giving the "objective tendencies" for certain "actual events" to occur. These "actual events" correspond to the particle-like aspects of nature, such as a photon striking a photographic plate and causing a crystal to blacken. This causes a real "collapse of the wave function," and a new, objective wave function for the

universe. As Stapp remarks, Heisenberg's ontology is only sketched briefly: "'Actual events' are characterized by the making of a permanent record (such as the mark on the photographic plate), but it is not clear under which circumstances actual events occur" (2004, pages 125-8). In *Mindful Universe* (2007, Chapter 13) Stapp links this Heisenberg ontology to the process philosophy of Alfred North Whitehead (1929), in which physics is regarded as being essentially about actual events occurring through time, and in which all of these actual events have proto-experiential as well as physical aspects.

Despite similarities, idealist panpsychism differs in three respects from the Heisenberg ontology. First, at least as understood by Whitehead and Stapp, the ultimates of the universe have both proto-experiential and physical aspects. In idealist panpsychism, the ultimates are entirely mind-like, but they do appear to one another as physical entities. Second, the Heisenberg ontology is at the level of physics whereas, as pictured in Figure 6.4, idealist panpsychism's ontology sits below the level of completed physics. Third, the ultimates of the Heisenberg ontology are momentary events (that is to say, it is a theory of process), whereas the ultimates of idealist panpsychism have been described here as corresponding to long-lived physical particles.

Notwithstanding these differences, I believe that the Heisenberg ontology could be adapted to throw light on idealist panpsychism. On point one, the advantage of insisting upon idealism is to avoid the misconception that there is any physical stuff in addition to the appearances of hierarchical systems of minds. Even Heisenberg's objective wave function of the universe is not to be interpreted as being "made of physical stuff", but is to be interpreted as Heisenberg describes. On point two, idealist panpsychism has advantages over the Heisenberg ontology in explaining both the mind-body relationship (Chapter 5) and mind-body causation (Chapter 6). On point three, the Heisenberg ontology has some advantages over idealist panpsychism. The latter theory would have to be adapted so as to become more process-like in order to account for the creation and destruction of particles.

2. What is it like to be a photon?

Consider a double slit experiment (Figure 3.1) in which the light source has been turned down so that only one photon is inside the apparatus at any time. According to idealist panpsychism, this photon is a fundamental experiential entity. It has a perspectival (subjective), qualitative experience of its environment. The environment is given by the particular experimental set-up. This ability to perceive is strong in the sense that it happens without regard to constraints of space or time (as evidenced by John Wheeler's "delayed choice" experiments: see Davies and Brown, 1986, pages 9-11 and 64-67).

A free choice made by the photon in the light of its experience determines the spot on the screen where it lands. The choice is wanton because the electron has no ability to think or reflect. The choice is not arbitrary, however, because if its experience had been different, as would have been the case if only one slit had been open, then a different set of propensities to make particular choices would have arisen.

An experimenter can calculate a probability distribution that describes the propensities for particular locations on the screen to be chosen. The fact that this distribution exists does not explain why this particular photon landed on this particular spot on this particular occasion. The *choice* made by a particular photon is still a legitimate explanation as to why it landed on this particular spot on the screen. An individual photon can make a free choice despite the fact that the collective pattern is random. This is because the probability distribution does not *constrain* each individual free choice made by each photon; instead it does no more than *describe* the collective pattern of these choices.

This needs bringing out in more detail. A process is *random* in terms of science if no additional observation is possible that might enable the experimenter to predict which particular outcome will be observed on any given run of the experiment. There is strong evidence that where the photon lands in the above example is random in this sense. It is crucial to understand that there is no contradiction between randomness thus defined and the photon having made free choice based on its sentience.

One might wish to counter by arguing for a stronger, metaphysical definition of randomness, in which an event is random if there is no cause whatsoever for it happening. Such metaphysical randomness clearly contradicts the notion of a photon having a free choice, because such a choice would be the cause of the observed outcome. I would reply that we have no reason to believe that events are random in this stronger metaphysical sense, and moreover nothing within science could provide any evidence for metaphysical randomness.

The choices discussed here, because they are based on unreflective, raw sentience, cannot amount to the free will experienced by humans. In Chapter 10 we will show that, in contrast, human free will depends upon the ability to think and to predict consequences.

3. What is it like to be a rock?
There are two broad camps of panpsychists. *Weak panpsychists* believe that an object as basic as a rock is merely an aggregate of the experiential entities (the molecules) that compose it. *Strong panpsychists* believe that the rock, considered as a whole, has extremely simple mental features, perhaps no more than the possession of raw percepts. Weak panpsychists have the task of explaining within their theory what it is that distinguishes an aggregate from a higher-level experiential being. Is a plant an

aggregate of cells, or is it an experiential being in its own right for instance? Strong panpsychists have the task of explaining the need for a rock to possess mind over and above the interacting minds of its constituents. Idealist panpsychism might be developed along either of these lines.

Panpsychists have been subject to much ridicule. What could it mean for a rock to have a mind, or to be composed of minds, no matter how simple? What purpose could these minds serve? After all, a rock's behavior is fully explained by the laws of physics, and nothing more needs to be said.

I believe that a case for panpsychism can be made from the way in which the quantum world and the classical world are linked (Bohm, 1951, Chapter 23). The classical world does not *arise* from the quantum world. Rather, in order for us to be able to investigate the quantum world, we have to *presume* that the classical world exists. However, we also want to give a reductive account of classical objects, such as rocks, in terms of their quantum constituents, such as electrons, quarks, and so on. This leads us into paradox. The Schrödinger equation applied to any system of elementary particles implies that they will smear out over a large region of space over time. When we observe a rock, it is never smeared out in space.

There are interpretations of quantum mechanics that suggest that the rock is indeed smeared out until it is observed. It would be more plausible, however, to have an account in which the rock is localized, even when we are not observing it. It is possible to sketch such an account, based on the Heisenberg ontology. The experiential entities that comprise the rock are in mutual interaction, and are observing one another. These interactions and observations lead to repeated collapses of the wave function of the rock, resulting in it remaining a solid object with a well-defined position in space. These mutual observations and collapses force the ultimate constituents of the rock to act in concert, so that the rock behaves as a near-classical object, rather than as a smear of quantum strangeness, even when we are not observing it.

In idealist panpsychism, all explanation must refer to the experiential layer (Figure 6.4). Above this layer we are only talking about appearances, and so there can only be the appearance of causation. It follows that even a complete *physical* explanation of the rock's behavior does not make the primitive mental features of the rock redundant. These mentalistic features have a function and purpose in preventing the rock from becoming smeared out – they are not epiphenomenal.

4. What is it like to be Schrödinger's cat?

With classical objects arising from quantum objects by collapses caused by self-observation, as in the example of the rock above, we have a natural, nearly-classical, realistic account of Schrödinger's cat. The cat in the chamber is in one nearly-classical state or another, and for the observer outside of the chamber, the wave function merely describes the knowledge of that state. Schrödinger's cat is just like any other "classical" cat.

According to the Heisenberg ontology, the past of the universe is fixed, and a wave function describes its open possibilities for the future. Between the past and the future there is a boundary demarking the "present moment". The universe moves towards the future in small, localized steps (these are literally quantum leaps). At each step the boundary moves, increasing the size of the fixed past in some localized, blister or bubble-like region (see Figure 8.1, based on Stapp, 2007, page 92). Each step represents a collective choice made by the group of experiential entities situated within the bubble. Between each step the wave function can be regarded a realistic expression of those entities' propensities to act. After each step, a new wave function for the universe becomes appropriate.

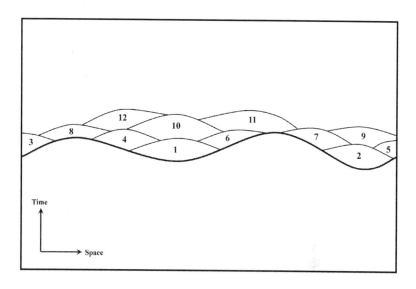

Figure 8.1: Development a small fragment of the universe over time (from time t to t+12)

Another observer, not one of the entities within the bubble, will not have access to their experiences nor to the information contained therein. This external observer can still use the original (uncollapsed) wave function to make useful predictions. For an external observer, the original wave function cannot be fully realistic. (For more detail about the Heisenberg ontology, see Stapp, 2007, Chapter 13.)

For example, for a particular entity, such as the crucial photon in the Schrödinger's cat experiment, its wave function encodes its propensities to make certain choices, and this function can thus be regarded realistically. Once the photon has made its choice, either breaking the phial of poison or harmlessly hitting the wall, a new state of the universe has arisen, and so a new wave function becomes appropriate. However, for someone outside the chamber, without knowledge of the choice, the original wave function is still appropriate as a tool to calculate probabilities of various outcomes.

According to idealist panpsychism and the Heisenberg ontology, what is actually going on inside the chamber is nearly classical. World lines of entities such as particles, rocks or cats are modeled as streams of bubbles of varying degrees of complexity. There is no large-scale, extreme quantum strangeness that would smear out the cat into a superposition of living and dead states.

Of course, this does not solve the measurement problem. Experiential entities must be making choices with sufficient rapidity that the inside of the chamber is quasi-classical, but these choices cannot be made with infinite rapidity, because we also know that the world is not perfectly classical. Beyond that we can presently say nothing.

5. What is it like to be a hydrogen atom?

Chapter 15 of *Quantum Theory* by David Bohm (1951) describes the electron orbiting the nucleus of a hydrogen atom in terms of cloud-like wave functions.

What might actually be going on in terms of idealist panpsychism? My highly speculative intuition is that, inside a hydrogen atom, the nucleus and the electron are observing each other, making position measurements with great rapidity. This would result in uncertainties in their momenta; but despite this, these repeated measurements would tend to hold the electron and nucleus near to one another, owing to what is called the quantum Zeno effect (Stapp, 2004, pages 253-5).

Doesn't this speculative (I am claiming more "realistic") picture contradict the standard picture given by wave functions? Not necessarily. The situation is similar to the Schrödinger's cat experiment, where the scientist outside the chamber uses a wave function to describe what is going on inside. This wave function does not accurately reflect the more-nearly-classical course of events inside the chamber, but it is nonetheless appropriate because the scientist does not have information about the quantum choices or events taking place inside the hidden chamber.

6. What is it like to be a brain?

Henry Stapp has given what is probably the most complete account of quantum mind in his two books *Mind, Matter and Quantum Mechanics* (second edition, 2004) and *Mindful Universe* (2007). The latter book is somewhat less technical, and includes a discussion of the social implications of his theories. According to Stapp, the brain contains within it *templates for action*. These are macroscopic states that will, if held for an extended period of time, cause an associated action to take place. Several highly distinct templates can exist in superposition. Two such templates might be to flee or to fight in the presence of a tiger (2007, Chapter 5).

Another crucial fact about the brain is that it comprises a complex network of neurons. Neurons work by means of electrical impulses traveling along their threadlike axons towards neighboring neurons. Neurons are not connected directly to one another: instead there is a small gap or synapse across which chemicals called neurotransmitters travel from one neuron to the next, carrying the signal. The functioning of the brain is thus electro-chemical rather than merely electrical.

In more detail: When the nerve impulse reaches the nerve terminal it opens up tiny ion channels in the terminal membrane. Calcium ions (waiting in the synapse) enter through these channels into the nerve terminal and release the neuro-transmitters, which then exit the nerve terminal and cross the synapse, transmitting the signal to the next neuron. The very small scale of the ion channels means that there is considerable quantum uncertainty as to whether or not a calcium ion entering the nerve terminal will succeed in playing its part in releasing the neurotransmitters. The probability that a nerve impulse will trigger the release of neurotransmitters is much less than 100%. This uncertainty is repeated throughout the brain making it uncertain as to which of the templates for action will be carried out (2007, pages 30-1).

Stapp crucially explains, with the aid of some useful schematic diagrams, why environmental decoherence does not ruin his model, reducing the brain to a single, purely classical state (2007, Chapter 11). First, decoherence eliminates quantum interference effects between quantum states that are "distant" from one another. Second, decoherence does not reduce the brain to a single classical state. Instead, the effect of decoherence is that *all possible classical states coexist in a mixture* with appropriate probabilities. States that are very "close" to one another can still interfere, so these coexisting, classical states must be regarded as being very slightly smeared out. These coexisting classical states would include both the fight and flight templates for action in the example above.

The remainder of Stapp's Chapter 11 is devoted to explaining how human beings make choices, and how these choices are reflected in the physical brain state. I will not go into further detail about Stapp's model here. Instead I recommend reading his *Mindful Universe* (2007).

Free will

An important feature of Stapp's account is that human choices are free in the extremely strong sense that there is no probability associated with them. This lack of a probability is consistent with our current state of knowledge of physics, but this might not be the case in the future.

On the contrary, suppose that the subject's brain state (or, more accurately, the subject's full ontological/experiential state) determines the probability of each of his or her possible actions. In Chapter 10 I hope to show that this more restrictive supposition is still consistent with human beings possessing genuine free will. Before that, the next chapter will face pain and suffering, and how such qualities are a necessary component of our free will.

9

Pain and Suffering

Pain isolates one. It pervades everything; blackens the sky, pushes other humans away, reduces music and poetry and the outside world to dullness; grinds on and on endlessly.

Joan Fitch in *Quaker Faith and Practice*
(Quaker, 1999, section 21.59)

Any theory of pain and suffering, if it is to be taken seriously, must be capable of accounting for experiences taken from ordinary lives, accurately described. Otherwise it is no more than a self-indulgent, intellectual game. The examples in this chapter are not untypical of many lives.

Ana María

One day in the summer of 1994 my wife Ana María suddenly collapsed in severe pain. She held on until I returned home from work, but we then immediately called for a doctor and she was taken to hospital. A few days later the surgeons operated. They found a large cyst and had to perform a total hysterectomy. This is a major operation, and Ana's recovery was slow and painful, taking many weeks.

We then settled back to life as usual. Stupidly I did not accompany her to the hospital to hear the result of the medical analysis. Ana María phoned me at work. The news was devastating for us both: she was diagnosed with cancer.

For the next four years Ana María suffered no more pain. She underwent various sequences of chemotherapy and other treatments. These were not painful, but she dreaded them because each session gave her severe nausea. We seemed to get into an awful routine. After each course of treatment Ana's cancer went into remission, but by the final six-month follow-up the cancer had invariably returned. At this point a new course of treatment would be suggested, either one that was already established, or a clinical trial. Chemotherapy works by poisoning the whole body, hence the nausea, but the poison is selected such that cancer cells are more susceptible to it. Some newer, experimental treatments were exciting in that they were more targeted. Ana María took part in a trial that involved being injected with molecules that had been made radioactive. These molecules flowed through the bloodstream and attached themselves to the cancerous cells, and so the radiation was concentrated most intensely on the tumor. "Targeted" is a relative term. I was only allowed to see Ana María in the isolated ward for brief periods of time, and I was supposed to keep well away from her on the other side of the room. For Ana even this treatment did not work.

With each course of treatment our hope became less and less. After the first couple of adverse follow-up reports we learned to keep our expectations very low, because to have our hopes raised and then dashed again was just too cruel, and forced us to repeat the suffering we had already struggled our way through. After about five years, and after about half a dozen courses of treatment, Ana María quietly but firmly told me that she would have no more treatments, but would have palliative care only. It was a realistic and rational decision.

The cancer was slowly spreading, and over the next couple of years Ana experienced ever-increasing pain. We would make occasional trips to the center of Oxford, and tour the chemists' shops buying up stocks of paracetamol [acetaminophen]. (In the UK, this can only legally be sold in very small quantities as a surprisingly effective measure to prevent suicide.) Eventually Ana María was maxing out on a cocktail of paracetamol and other painkillers. Her pain was unceasing and she tried to carry out her everyday tasks through it, but a wave would suddenly catch her. She would frequently scream and double over in agony, and the very act of doing this would make her pain worse. Our GP recommended that she needed to go onto liquid morphine, and arranged for us to visit a hospice where this could be initiated.

Morphine has properties in the treatment of pain that are either marvelous or dreadful depending on your outlook. It does not work at all for some people. For those for whom it works, there is no set dose, and one person can need to take ten or twenty times as much as another. If you exceed the dose that relieves your pain, and continuously increase it, you will first become drowsy, then comatose and finally you will die. The person whose pain is relieved by a small dose of morphine would certainly be killed by taking the twenty times higher dose needed by another patient. For this reason, when starting to take morphine, it is necessary to begin with a very small dose and gradually increase it until pain diminishes to a level "acceptable" to the patient.

Ana María's going onto morphine was the most dreadful and wretched part of her illness. It was far worse than her eventual dying. Her painkillers were withdrawn, and she was put on a minimal dose of morphine. She was in agony. The dose was gradually increased over a period of about three months until her pain had diminished. The doctors and nurses in the hospice (and also our GP) were magnificent in helping her through this period. Once the correct dosage of morphine was reached, we found it to be a great blessing. Ana María still experienced a great deal of pain, but never to same the crippling extent. She was again able to take other pain medication in conjunction with the morphine, and was able to carry on her life more or less as normal. We were continuously trying to adjust the morphine dose up and down to find the optimum. Sometimes Ana would decrease the dose so that, although this increased the pain, she would be awake enough to carry out a particular activity such as meeting friends. Her endurance was such that shortly before her death I asked her a question about pain, expecting her to tell me that it only troubled her occasionally. I was devastated when she told me that she had been in constant pain for the past two years.

Daniel Dennett on pain

In his influential book *Consciousness Explained* (1991) Daniel Dennett argues that *qualia* – experiential, qualitative feelings or mental states such as pain or nausea – do not exist. He goes out of his way to ridicule philosophers who think that they do, and he describes laypeople's belief that they have pains as being a deluded, naive folk theory. Dennett claims that what we deludedly perceive as pains are in reality no more that mechanistic processes in the brain resulting from damage to the organism. It is hard to summarize Dennett's argument towards this conclusion as he spends twelve chapters arguing for it. You will have to read the whole of his book.

In common with all laypeople, and together with the philosophical opponents of Dennett (notably Chalmers 1996, and Searle 2004), I deny that experiential qualities are theoretical constructs, and so in particular they cannot be ill-defined theoretical constructs. Instead, like Chalmers and Searle, I take qualia to be basic facts about our mental lives that call for an explanation.

On page 61 of his book, Dennett asks the key question, "**But why do pains have to *hurt* so much?**" However, he never gets around to answering this in a clear and concise manner. He agrees that we *seem* to have pains, but in his theory pains must somehow be delusional because an actual pain could not feature in any physicalist explanation, and physicalist explanations are the only explanations that he recognizes.

In a later paper Dennett tries to answer this key question succinctly:

In creatures as cognitively complex as us (with our roughly inexhaustible capacity for meta-reflections and higher order competitions between policies, meta-policies, etc.), the 'blood is about to be lost sensors' and their kin cannot simply be 'hooked up to the right action paths'... In us there is an informationally sensitive *tug-of war, which leaves many traces, provokes many reflections (about the detailed awfulness of it all), permits many protocols (and poignant complaints), adjusts many behavioural propensities (such as desires to reform one's ways, or seek revenge), lays down many ('false') memories about the way the pain felt, etc., etc.*

Daniel Dennett (1992, page 323)

Dennett regards us as biological machines (1991, pages 431-2), but how could information encoded in a machine of any type be "about detailed awfulness," "poignant," or about "desires"? There is no awfulness, poignancy or desire in any machine, whereas these words emotively suggest that there is. It is confused and confusing language.

The most important confusion comes in the final line where he claims that this information processing "lays down many ('false') memories about the way the pain felt." According to Dennett, pains are at most mechanistic processes in the brain resulting from damage to the organism, but "the way the pain felt" can only mean the experiential quality of pain, which for Dennett *does not exist*. So, what is the memory *about*? Moreover, what sort of "memory" is Dennett referring to? For him it can only be analogous to the kind of memory found in a computer: the physical recording of information. It cannot be the kind of memory we humans have, in which there is something it is like to remember a pain, because for Dennett qualitative experiences of any kind do not exist. Dennett's term "('false')", enclosing his f-word in both scare quotes and parentheses, takes the art of weasel words to new depths. Is the memory true or false?

Dennett's claim (1991, pages 431-2) that we are machines stretches the word beyond any possible useful meaning. The word "machine" should be reserved for a computer or robot-like entity, and there is no evidence that we function in this manner. When a machine retrieves a "('false') memory about the way the pain felt," does this amount to an experienced pain? Or to an experienced memory of an experienced pain? Or even a delusion of an experienced memory of an experienced pain? No. It is like nothing at all, because there is nothing it is like to be a machine. The idea that machines can have experiences is, as David Hodgson says, a superstition. Dennett has failed to explain why pains hurt at all.

Galen Strawson is scathing about Dennett's and others' denial of the reality of experiences such as pain. He points out that, "for there to *seem to be* rich phenomenology or experience *just is for there to be* such phenomenology or experience," (my emphasis). He also says:

> *I think we should feel very sober, and a little afraid, at the power*
> *of human credulity, the capacity of human minds to be gripped*
> *by theory, by faith. For this particular denial is the strangest*
> *that has ever happened in the whole history of human thought,*
> *not just the whole history of philosophy. It falls, unfortunately,*
> *to philosophy, not religion, to reveal the greatest woo-woo of the*
> *human mind. I find this grievous ..*

Strawson (2006, pages 5-6)

Dennett on suffering

Dennett begins an account of the relationship between pain and suffering by approvingly quoting philosopher Jeremy Bentham:

> "A full-grown horse or dog is beyond comparison a more rational, as well as a more conversible animal than an infant of a day or a week, or even a month old. But

suppose they were otherwise, what would it avail? The question is not, Can they *reason*? nor, Can they *talk*, but Can they *suffer*?"

(in Dennett, 1991, page 449).

Dennett goes on to give his own account of suffering:

Suffering is not a matter of being visited by some ineffable but intrinsically awful state, but of having one's life hopes, life plans, life projects blighted by circumstances imposed on one's desires, thwarting one's intentions – whatever they are. The idea of suffering being somehow explicable as the presence of some intrinsic property – horribility let's say – is as hopeless as the idea of amusement being somehow explicable as the presence of intrinsic hilarity... It follows... that the capacity to suffer is a function of the capacity to have articulated, wide-ranging, highly discriminative desires, expectations, and other sophisticated mental states.

Dennett (1991, page 449)

Dennett goes on to say: "Human beings are not the only creatures smart enough to suffer; Bentham's horse and dog show by their behavior that they have enough mental complexity to distinguish – and care about – a spectrum of pains and other indispositions that is far from negligible..."

Dennett is suggesting that he and Bentham have identical views, but this is far from being the case. Bentham did believe that pains existed as experiential qualities that caused suffering. No one in the eighteenth century was sufficiently deluded by his or her philosophy into denying the experiential reality of pain. So when Bentham asks the rhetorical question, "Can they suffer?" this is short for "Can they suffer owing to this pain experience?" Bentham is explicitly *contrasting* the fact of suffering pain with the possession of intellectual capacity. He would agree that there is also a kind of intellectual suffering that is linked to cognitive ability, and which is related to blighted hopes as Dennett describes, but this is not the kind of suffering that Bentham is talking about. When Bentham talks about suffering in the above quotation, he means suffering from pain.

Bentham was arguing that we owe a moral duty to animals to the extent that they experience (suffer) pain. The highly intellectual type of suffering that Dennett describes really only applies to adult humans: even Bentham's most "conversible" horse comes nowhere near meeting Dennett's definition of suffering, as you will see if you plug a horse into Dennett's definition: horses do not have any "life hopes, life plans, life projects"(!) to be blighted.

The contrast between Dennett and Bentham becomes clear when we consider the example of a baby. Bentham clearly believes that babies can suffer pain despite neither being able to reason nor talk. For Dennett, babies do not feel pain because there is no such thing as the experiential quality of pain. Nor do babies suffer, for they cannot satisfy his definition of suffering.

According to Dennett, suffering (despite his talk of "hopes") is a purely functional and behavioral concept, without any experiential quality. Given this wildly implausible view, it is difficult to understand why we ought to act to prevent suffering.

Simon Weston

Simon Weston was a Welsh Guardsman during the 1982 Falklands war. He was no further than 20 feet from a 2000 lb bomb that exploded, engulfing him in the fireball, and killing 22 out of the 30 men of his mortar platoon. He describes his experiences:

> Suddenly everybody sprang back to life, but now men were shadows, silhouettes with brilliant, whole-body haloes of the most beautiful colours I had ever seen – a sunburst that I could

touch and yet couldn't touch: it was touching me, I couldn't touch back. I felt the air sucked from my lungs and then a surge of hot air washed over me. No sensation yet of the cruel, excruciating, unrelenting heat: in the first blinding flash all my exposed nerve-endings had been scorched away...

Pain drew my eyes to the backs of my hands and I watched, transfixed by horror, as they fried and melted, the skin flaking and bubbling away from the bone like the leaves of a paperback burning on a bonfire before being carried away by the wind...

It got worse...

Simon Weston (1989, pages 146-8)

He went through many more horrors before he escaped the flames, not least seeing many of his comrades die in obscene ways. At one point he screamed for a gun so that he could kill himself. His face was so badly burned that on his return to the UK, his mother, who was expecting to meet him and knew of his injuries, did not recognize him (page 181). He describes his later treatment:

My body was forty-six percent burned, and all the affected areas needed to be resurfaced with fresh skin. What I had thought of as my unscarred areas rapidly became donor sites for the areas that were badly burned. And let me tell you, having just one split-skin graft of one part of me that I'd thought had escaped the inferno was bad enough. Having that area and other areas harvested again and again for yet more skin was absolutely excruciating, and meant that those areas too became scarred... The agony of the operations had only just begun.

(page 188)

Much later on he goes on to say:

I discovered that my biggest battle of all was just beginning –

the fight for rehabilitation. The physical pain might have gradually lessened, but emotional pain was about to take its place – just as intense, and just as unbearable.

(page 197)

If Dennett's theory of suffering is correct, then Simon Weston shouldn't mind his raw flesh being harvested; on the contrary, he should enjoy seeing his prospects improve. In a similar vein, why would Dennett want to have an anesthetic when undergoing dental treatment? After all, this treatment will not cause him any harm, and will improve his teeth.

Dennett's supposed account of pain does not acknowledge the fact of pain. His account of suffering is inadequate as a result. He deals only with purely intellectual suffering, and not at all with physical suffering such as is described above.

The medical profession

Professor of psychology Ronald Melzack gives a realistic, rational, and compassionate account of human pain and suffering:

Pain is not simply a function of the amount of bodily damage alone, but is influenced by attention, anxiety, suggestion, prior experience and other psychological variables...

Pain is a complex perceptual and affective experience determined by the unique past history of the individual, by the meaning to him of the injurious agent or situation, and by his 'state of mind' at the moment, as well as by the sensory nerve patterns evoked by physical stimulation...

The subjective experience of pain clearly has sensory qualities, such as are described by the words throbbing, burning, or sharp. In addition it has distinctly unpleasant, affective qualities which are described by words such as exhausting, wretched and punishing. Pain becomes overwhelming, demands immediate attention, and disrupts ongoing behaviour and thought. It motivates or drives the organism into activity aimed at stopping the pain as quickly as possible.

In Richard Gregory (Ed., 1987, pages 574-5)

In the article Melzack describes a multi-faceted approach to pain control involving medication, acupuncture, electrical nerve stimulation, and psychological techniques such as biofeedback, hypnosis, imagery, and distraction. He describes pain clinics, palliative care units and hospices as representing a major break-through of the highest importance in the clinical control of pain.

As Melzack shows, health care professionals do not attempt to solve the philosophical mind-body problem; instead they take the facts of pain and suffering as given, and use them to develop a humane and rational treatment package.

David Hodgson on pain

David Hodgson's thesis is that pain is closely associated with free will. He writes clearly and compactly, with each phrase rich in meaning. I only appreciated the full content of his words when typing out the following quotation. I recommend that you write it out for yourself, or at least read it aloud (emphasis in the original):

My contention is that pain, as such, in giving us notice of possible damage and a motive to remedy it and avoid future damage, has an irreducible *role; because it leaves us with a* choice *to do something else if we decide other reasons should prevail. This only makes sense if choices are not just the working out of mechanisms obeying universal laws or computa-tional rules, but really do require a conscious agent who can treat both the pain and the opposing considerations as non-conclusive, and reach a decision which then, for the first time, determines which considerations are to prevail on that unique occasion.*

If, as I believe, there are advantages which a faculty for (fallible) qualitative judgement has over purely quantitative computation, then the role and usefulness of pain can be understood.

David Hodgson (1996, pages 72-3)

For me this is a highly plausible account of the advantage of pain over mechanism in allowing for free, well-considered actions in difficult situations. Simon Weston's attempt to save one of his comrades despite the pain of his flesh being stripped from his hands illustrates Hodgson's theory; as does the courage of many people in repeatedly facing the nausea of chemotherapy. This leads on to the next chapter's topic, which is free will. First I wish to give another example.

Dining out

By the Christmas of 2002, Ana María was bedridden, with many periods of intense pain, and it was clear to us both that she had only a very short time to live. She insisted that she wanted to go out for one final meal with her friends, and she would not be persuaded against this plan. On 27 December therefore Ana María and I, together with our friends Roger and Elizabeth, went out for lunch at a restaurant in Oxford. Ana had slept all morning to give herself strength, and took only a little morphine so as to stay alert. Getting Ana into the taxi was a struggle, even though it was parked only a couple of meters from our front door.

When we arrived at the restaurant it was even worse. There is a pedestrian crossing immediately in front of the entrance, and the driver refused to pull up on top of it. As a result, I had to take Ana's arm around my shoulder and with my other arm around her waist drag her the twenty meters to the entrance. Ana was staggering and collapsing, and the short walk took us ages. It was like struggling to climb a huge mountain, with the frightening prospect of falling or not being able to go further. Neither of my friends was able to help as one had an injured hip, and the other was frail. Once inside we insisted on being seated at once. Ana María slumped in her seat, but recovered enough to order. She rested, almost sleeping, while we waited for the food to arrive.

Once the food was served, Ana became lively and animated. She was clearly enjoying herself and she participated fully in our conversations. I was also amazed that she managed to eat a substantial proportion of her meal. We were fathoms deep in love, and had splendid food and brilliant company. It was a wonderful, magical time together.

The journey home was, as I feared, a nightmarish repeat of the outward trip. I dragged Ana María to the bed that was made up for her downstairs and she fell asleep immediately, fully clothed. She spent all of the following day and night comatose, after which she recovered a little. She died on 1 January 2003.

10

Free Will

This afternoon I may choose to stop working earlier than usual to take my two kids for a walk in the woods. But just how free would such a choice be? Each supposedly free act is the culmination of an infinite sequence of proximate and long-range causes. Quantum mechanics and chaos theory suggests that pinpointing the causes might be extremely difficult, even impossible, but that does not mean the causes do not exist. Retracing the steps that led to a particular act takes us back into childhood and the womb, back through the history of Homo sapiens *and of all life on earth, and finally to the big bang itself, the creation event that supposedly set everything in motion. I didn't ask for any of this, so how free can I be?*

John Horgan, (1999, page 247)

John Horgan eloquently expresses the dilemma of free will. He would like to take credit for being a good parent, but he can only validly do so if the decision to take his children for a walk is genuinely and ultimately to some extent his responsibility. It is certainly the case that John's genetics and upbringing would have influenced his brain state, and thus the probability that he would come to one decision rather than another. His biology, upbringing and present environment will influence his priorities. Nonetheless, for his self-understanding as an ethical agent, it is essential that, after reflection, he can finally make a choice that has some component of genuine freedom notwithstanding these influences. It is not sufficient to make a so-called "choice" that is fully determined by the physics of his brain and of the world.

Many subtle factors come into play in any discussion of free will. What do we mean by "choice" or "random" for instance? This chapter will investigate these technicalities.

Two contrasting viewpoints

There are two highly contrasting views that can be taken of a human being. The first is as a person who can make genuine, effective choices in the light of his or her experiences. (Choices clearly have limitations – a person cannot choose to jump a mile high.) The second is as a physical system developing according to precise laws. This chapter gives explicit statements of these contrasting viewpoints, and goes on to explain how these two viewpoints are reconciled under idealist panpsychism. These viewpoints are:

Libertarian free will (FW): In our everyday lives, we are all of us convinced that we are the ultimate authors and originators of at least some of our actions. This conviction is essential to our self-understanding as human beings. Surely, we think, the relationships we achieve, the particular words we speak or write, the things we make, the songs we sing, the children we bring into the world, the projects and activities we undertake are in part an expression of our thoughts and feelings. To this extent, our actions are our responsibility, and are ultimately brought about, at least in part, by the decisions we make as persons. From the point of view we usually take in everyday life, the idea that our choices, based on our phenomenal experiences, thoughts and beliefs, can influence our behavior and thus alter the course of events in the world seems entirely natural, unmysterious and unproblematic.

Physical system (PS): Another picture we have of ourselves is as physical systems, made out of the same materials (molecules, atoms and ultimates such as electrons), and obeying the same laws, as any other object in nature. Our development over time is determined by mathematically precise physical laws that operate, if not deterministically, then at least probabilistically. Current physics can only deal with simple systems, but one would hope and believe that completed physics (discussed in Chapter 3) would have the following character: For any physical system, in given state P_1, and in given environment E, then for each possible subsequent state P_2, there would exist a mathematically definite probability p that the system would move to P_2.

The question arises: which, if either, of these two highly contrasting viewpoints is right? For example, consider a president sitting in his office deciding whether or not to sign an order now that will take his country to war. Regarded as a physical system, the president is in a physical state P_1, which importantly includes his brain state. In our completed physics, there must be a mathematically definite probability p that he will sign the document before getting up from the desk. Regarded as a person, however, the president is making a genuinely free choice, for which he is ultimately responsible.

In this chapter I will argue that these contrasting viewpoints, FW and PS, are reconcilable, and that both are literally true. In the definition of PS, it is irrelevant that probabilities such as p are far beyond any conceivable way of being calculated. The assumption made throughout this chapter is that such probabilities invariably exist. Making this assumption gives the strongest possible statement of PS. If we can show that PS and FW are reconcilable under this assumption, then they will also be reconcilable without it.

The view of a person sketched in the FW paragraph requires genuine (technically called libertarian) free will. The first task is to clarify the concept of libertarian free will.

Robert Kane's model of free will

Robert Kane gives a detailed account of the issues surrounding the concept of free will (1998). These are more complex and subtle than one might imagine. The aspect of free will most immediately illustrated by the president's decision is called alternative possibilities. In Kane's words:

> **(AP):** *The agent has* alternative possibilities *(or can do otherwise) with respect to* [action] *A at* [time] *t in the sense that, at t, the agent can (has the power or ability to) do A and can (has the power or ability to) do otherwise.*
>
> Kane (1998, page 33)

Kane gives a detailed account of the issues between libertarians and compatibilists, who interpret AP differently from one another. He points out that arguments about alternative possibilities often end in an unproductive stalemate. *Libertarians* (believers in genuine free will) say that phrases such as "could have done otherwise" should be taken literally.

Compatibilists, who try to reinterpret free will so as to make it compatible with determinism, take the words "could have done otherwise" conditionally, writing them instead as "I would have done otherwise, if I had desired or believed/thought otherwise." This change of "could" into "would" seems to me and to many libertarians to be shifty and evasive. If, as compatibilists contend, my brain state is such that I am bound to choose the apple pie, then it is useless to assert that I would have chosen ice cream if my brain state had been different. The fact is that I am not in an ice cream brain state, and so there is no possibility of me eating ice cream.

At the start of the chapter, John Horgan expressed his ambiguity about free will in the context of taking his children for a walk. As a good father, he would like to think of himself as a libertarian who freely chooses to spend time with his kids. As a scientist, he believes that the proximate cause of his choice was brought about by his current brain state ("I would have done otherwise, if I had desired or believed/thought otherwise"), and that this chain of causality can be followed right back to the big bang. In other words, he believes that science forces him to be a compatibilist. I want to show that he is mistaken, and that libertarian free will is consistent with science.

Kane believes that there is a difference in world-view that underlies these disagreements about free will that needs to be brought into the open. The difference is that libertarians believe that humans have ultimate responsibility for some of their actions, whereas compatibilists do not. He shows many examples of philosophical disputes about different aspects of free will where this hidden assumption has lead to stalemate. Kane's definition of ultimate responsibility is complex, and factors into two parts: (R) responsibility, and (U) ultimacy.

Here is his definition in full:

(UR): *An agent is* ultimately responsible *for some (event or state) E's occurring only if*

(R): *The agent is personally responsible for E's occurring in a sense which entails that something the agent voluntarily (or willingly) did or omitted, and for which the agent could voluntarily have done otherwise, either was, or causally contributed to, E's occurrence and made a difference to whether or not E occurred; and*

(U): *For every X and Y (where X and Y represent occurrences of events and/or states) if the agent is personally responsible for X, and if Y is an* arche *(or sufficient ground or cause or explanation) for X, then the agent must also be personally responsible for Y.*

Kane (1998, page 35)

Elsewhere, in a simplified account of his ideas, Kane explains that, in order to have ultimate responsibility for E, an agent must be at least partly responsible for anything that is a sufficient reason (condition, cause or motive) for the E occurring (2002). This idea of UR brings a historical dimension to the concept of free will: the fact that we are free at this moment depends not only on our current physical (especially brain) state, but on the fact that we arrived at this state by a process of living through earlier experiences and decisions. This crucial historical dimension will be discussed more fully later.

Throughout this chapter I will be taking Kane's libertarian position, which defines FW in terms of both AP and UR; and where AP is taken literally. These conditions are a detailed explication of the definition of FW given above.

Mind-body causation

Libertarian free will presupposes the reality of genuine conscious choices and thus of mind-body causation, and this we need to look at again.

A common academic attitude towards consciousness is that it must be an epiphenomenon. However, Daniel Dennett (1991) has given a decisive argument against epiphenomenal consciousness. He has compared qualia (experiential qualities or feelings) to gremlins, arguing that, because they have no effect whatsoever, they should be dismissed as nonsense. If qualia were indeed epiphenomenal, then there would be no rational reason for believing in them. Dennett concludes that qualia do not exist. His argument goes like this:

1. There is no place in physics for mind-body causation
2. Thus qualia, if they exist, cannot have any effect on the course of the world
3. Claimed entities which have no effect on the course of the world cannot be real
4. Thus qualia do not exist

There are two major weaknesses in Dennett's argument. First, in his justification for step 1, he depends crucially on the assumption that we are living in an essentially classical world. He admits that quantum effects do exist, but assumes without further investigation that these have no relevance to brain function. Second, from our own personal experience, we all have to regard sensations such as toothache as being real, and their particular quality (here painfulness) as being the essence of what they are. As part of a longer argument against Dennett's position, Galen Strawson says:

> Could there be no experience or consciousness at all?... The answer "No" comes quickly and correctly, as it came to Descartes. What is it to suppose that one might be completely wrong? It is to suppose that although it seems to me that there is experience – for this cannot be denied – there actually isn't any experience. But this is an immediate reductio ad absurdum. For this seeming is already experience.
>
> Strawson (1994, page 51)

Because of these weaknesses, Dennett's argument about epiphenomena should be reversed, while preserving the valid points that he makes, as follows:

1. Human experience tells us that qualia are real
2. Claimed entities that have no effect on the course of the world cannot be real
3. Therefore qualia must have an effect on the course of the world
4. Everything that exists must eventually be describable in a way compatible with physics
5. Therefore qualia must be describable in a way compatible with physics
6. There is no way that qualia can have an effect in terms of

classical physics

7. Therefore qualia must be describable in terms compatible with non-classical physics

In more detail: Point 1 is Descartes' thesis that human experiences are central to who we are and what we know ourselves to be: see Chapters 4 and 9. Point 2 is Dennett's decisive argument against epiphenomena. Point 3 is a conclusion from points 1 and 2. It is a strong assertion about the reality of mind-body causation, but one which is in accord with commonsense intuitions and everyday language use: someone who says "I have a toothache" is engaged in a physical action which is telling us about a pain. Point 4 is universally accepted. Point 5 follows from points 1 and 4. Point 6 is widely accepted, for example, both by Dennett and by Stapp (2004a, pages 39, 138). The argument is technically complex, but boils down to the fact that in classical physics matter changes its configuration deterministically, and so there is neither need nor room for causation by qualia. In point 7, the term non-classical physics is to be construed broadly, but the paradigm example of such a theory is quantum mechanics.

An account of mind-body causation in terms of idealist panpsychism has already been given in Chapter 6.

Physical systems

Next we turn to the definition of a physical system (PS) given above, and clarify and motivate the definition. The main point of contention is whether or not we should expect a mathematically definite probability p to exist, especially in the complex situation where P_1 is the physical state (including brain state) of a president in his office deciding whether or not to take his country to war.

Of course, as already noted, for objects as complex as humans, there is no conceivable way to calculate probability p.

Henry Stapp's opinion is important, because his theory of quantum mind, discussed in Chapter 8, provides the specific and authoritative physical buttressing of the philosophy of idealist panpsychism given here. His provisional opinion is that p does not exist. He points out that within quantum theory, there are presently no known laws (not even probabilistic laws) within his theory that govern choices made by physicists (2004a, pages 242-5). He connects this lawlessness as having consequences for human freedom, although he admits, "It is not ruled out that some deeper theory will eventually provide a causal explanation of this 'choice'."

An important argument for PS is that consciousness has evolved. Stapp and I agree that (phenomenal) consciousness is causally effective, and that this causal effectiveness is associated with free choices. Moreover, human consciousness and freedom are highly sophisticated and structured, and so must have a long evolutionary history from primitive precursors. If human freedom is lawless, in the sense of being free even from probabilities, then the question arises as to how and when did such lawless freedom emerge? Evolution is a theory of process that requires the universe to proceed from state to state with well-defined probabilities. If lawlessness was present at the beginning, then evolution could not happen because the concept of fitness would not have any meaning. If lawlessness were a sudden late development, it would seem to be a miracle that evolution developed in a direction to a point where creatures, say hominids, developed a novel, lawless freedom, by virtue of some feature of their brain structure.

It is possible to argue that such lawless freedom emerged gradually, and coevolved with sentience, until we arrive at humans possessing sophisticated consciousness and lawless freedom. As a creature evolved with increasing sentience, it would initially have lawless freedom in only a limited number of environmental situations. Later on the scope of the environments in which it was lawlessly free would increase. Such an emergent lawlessness is rejected here because it puts the biology of sentient creatures beyond science, with science breaking down as sentience evolves. This is an unattractive (but not impossible) position to hold. With PS, on the other hand, it is true that, in principle at least, biological science applies to every living thing, including creatures as complex as presidents.

In this book, I accept Stapp's theory of quantum mind, but reject his provisional claim that lawlessness is essential to libertarian free will.

Stapp and panpsychism

Since I lean so heavily on Henry Stapp's work I had better explain that he denies that he is a panpsychist. I believe that this is a mere verbal difference, in that he uses terms like "mind", "consciousness" and "panpsychism" in much narrower ways than I have defined them here. Stapp prefers to base his theory on human consciousness, because this is the best-understood case, and generally to avoid speculation outside of this context as being premature.

Some of Stapp's statements, however, lean towards panpsychism, as this term is commonly (and broadly) understood. For example, he says, "These considerations motivate the first basic proposal of this work, which is to attach to each Heisenberg actual event an experiential aspect," (2004a, page 151). According to the Heisenberg ontology, such events comprise the totality of events that occur in the universe. Stapp's proposal is thus very close to an assertion of panpsychism. Moreover he says:

> *The physical world thus becomes an evolving structure of information, and of propensities for experiences to occur, rather than a mechanically evolving mindless material structure. The new conception essentially fulfils the age-old philosophical idea that*

nature should be made out of a kind of stuff that combines in an integrated and natural way certain mind-like and matter-like qualities, without being reduced to either classically conceived mind or classically conceived matter.

Stapp (2004a, page 268)

The ideas of Whitehead (1978) are seminal for the variant of panpsychism being proposed here, although his writing style is opaque. His ideas have been expressed with great clarity by Griffin (1998). Whitehead says:

"Actual entities" – also termed "actual occasions" are the final things of which the world is made up. There is no going behind actual entities to find anything more real... these actual entities are drops of experience...

Whitehead (1978, page 18)

These are clearly somewhat analogous to Heisenberg's actual events, and Stapp, when attaching to each actual event an experiential aspect, speaks of the "Whitehead-Heisenberg ontology" (2004a, page 81). Whitehead's claim is that "each actuality is essentially bipolar – physical and mental," (2004a, page 108) and "prehension" is his term for the experiential aspect by which matter "feels" its environment. Whitehead agrees that this experiential aspect must be causally effective if it is to be considered real. He expresses this in the terminology of Locke, "The chief ingredient in the notion of 'substance' is the notion of 'power,'" (1978, page 56). Stapp sums up this ontology, "All that exists is created by a sequence of creative acts or events, each of which brings into being one possibility from the multitude created by prior acts," (2004a, page 81).

Idealist panpsychism and free will

Now that the decks have been cleared, we can begin to answer

the question: *How does idealist panpsychism reconcile FW with PS?*
The answer can be given under several headings.

- ## The PS picture arises from the fundamental FW ontology

According to idealist panpsychism, physics, even completed
physics, deals only with appearances. In actuality and in essence
a human being is a hierarchy of experiential entities – as is any
physical object. So PS and FW are consistent despite their
different descriptions. FW describes human beings as they are in
themselves, whereas PS describes the appearance of this
actuality to others.

- ## All causation is at the fundamental, ontological (FW) level of experiential entities, and is between experiential entities

It is often claimed that the physical world is causally closed in
the sense that all causation is at the level of completed physics.
According to idealist panpsychism, however, there is no
ontology at the level of physics, and so no causation whatsoever
at that level. The appearance of physical causation, and of the
strict regularities we call "physical laws", arise from actual
causation at the experiential level, as can be seen in Figure 6.4.

- ## All causation between experiential entities is in terms of qualified free choices, based on experience

The choices are qualified because there are constraints necessary
for the consistency of physics. If a photon is to interact with an
electron for example, then the electron must interact with the
photon. There are also constraints on freedom because, in any
given situation, some hierarchies of experiential entities can be

regarded as being in competition or in cooperation with another hierarchy, and some will have greater ability to proceed undisturbed. In the case of a bullet hitting flesh, for example, the flesh will be forced to give way.

- **In any given experiential situation, the probability p that a particular qualified free choice will be made is mathematically definite, even if unknowable**

This statement effectively moves the probability p from statement PS into statement FW. Another way of putting this is to say that, in Figure 6.4, probability p effectively moves from the level of physics to the foundational experiential level. This move is needed so that the qualified free choice based on thoughts, beliefs and experiences does not violate the laws of completed physics. If there were no mathematically definite probabilities at the fundamental experiential level, then there could be no probabilities at the level of physics.

- **In idealist panpsychism, consciousness does not distort quantum probabilities**

For example, David Papineau has written:

> Still, this quantum mechanical indeterminism doesn't really help dualism. As long as prior physical causes so much as fix the probabilities of physical results, independent mental influences will still be ruled out.
>
> Imagine, for the sake of argument, that independent conscious events − conscious decisions perhaps − did take advantage of the indeterministic space created by quantum mechanics to influence the movements of neurotransmitters in the brain. Then presumably such neurotransmitter movements would occur more often when preceded by those conscious

decisions than when not.

Papineau & Selina (2000, pages 74-5)

Papineau's quote does not count against idealist panpsychism because panpsychists regard *all* actual (quantum) events as *constituting* choices based on sentience. Sentience and choice do not modify quantum probabilities; rather, *they are everywhere the explanation of how these probabilities arise.* Sentience and choice are ubiquitous throughout the universe. Certain of these feelings, namely those in the human brain occurring at the executive level of forming templates for action, are associated with the stream of human consciousness, and the corresponding choices constitute human free will.

How can a choice made with mathematically definite probability p be truly free: isn't it just random like the toss of a coin? I will answer this question over the remainder of the chapter.

A human person

The ideas given so far can be brought together to provide a coherent picture of what it is to be a human person.

Externally, the life of a person can be recognized as their world line, from their moment of birth, up until the present moment. Internally each person's history can be recognized as a stream of experiences, and of the particular choices made in the light of those experiences. In Stapp's model, there is no need to assume an ontologically separate "viewer" of experiences or "maker" of choices, either of which would lead to an infinite regress, see Stapp (2004a, page 21). Kane says:

At crunch time, the agents just do it, they settle indecision, respond to indeterminacy, and take responsibility then and there for setting their lives on one or another future branching pathway.

Kane (1998, page 193)

All choices, including important life choices such as the president's decision, are made in the light of the present moment of experience. Somehow this moment must encapsulate sufficient knowledge about the president, the world, and the likely consequences of each possible act, in order that the action can be to some degree rational and coherent. This implies that there is some kind of unity and holistic character to each moment of experience. This is true even without making the further, false claim that this experience perfectly matches the true state of the world.

The president's choice is a complex one, and would involve a whole sequence of choices while mulling over the issue: which factors are important and which can be neglected? How does one weigh loss of national prestige against loss of life? (Here "weigh" is an inadequate metaphor for a process of conscious judgment. This involves seeing each possible future situation as a whole rather than arbitrarily assigning a numerical value to each possibility.) Will backing down now make a more dangerous war more likely in the future? And so on. This thought process involves many choices, but at the end of it a final, decisive choice must be made.

As we saw in Chapter 8, an entangled quantum mechanical state constitutes a single, holistic, information rich state that is shared as a unit by a system of many particles. Such a state is thus ideal for representing the present moment in a person's stream of consciousness; see Seager (1995, pages 282-4), and Stapp (2004a, pages 9-12). Writing in 1890 William James likened consciousness to a continuously flowing river or stream, rather than a discrete chain or train of thought (1983, page 233). He also made clear the holistic character of our conscious experience at each present moment:

The next point to make clear is that, however complex the object may be, the thought of it is one undivided state of consciousness...

There is no manifold of coexisting ideas; the notion of such a thing is a chimera. Whatever things are thought in relation are thought from the outset in a unity, a single pulse of subjectivity, a single psychosis, feeling, or state of mind.

James (1983, pages 266, 268)

Henry Stapp agrees, "But a conscious thought is a real thing that has an *essential unity*. It is not merely an aggregation of simpler parts. It is fundamentally one whole thing," (2004a, page 137).

The initial movements of a baby's limbs are haphazard, and not under the baby's control. By observing and laying down in memory the results of its willful acts (Stapp, 2004a, page 129), the baby gradually, over many repeated experiments, comes to have control of its limbs. Human beings are characterized by having a lengthy childhood, and during play, they have ample time to experiment and discover the consequences of their actions in ever more complex situations. They lay down memories and are co-creators in forming their own characters as persons.

Human free will develops over the course of childhood. By extended experiential and experimental play, the baby learns the consequences of throwing food on the floor, or putting it in its mouth. The idea that food is in general good to eat is one basic template for action. Except in tragically deprived instances, babies grow to young adults in a supportive environment, where they learn a multitude of ever more sophisticated templates. This long childhood history is essential for our developing free will. Even as adults, our free will is not perfect, but continues as we develop wisdom during the unfolding of our adult lives. Robert Kane writes:

Another kind of disservice is done by continuing to appeal to a mysterious form of agency to account for free will... This can easily lead one to think in turn that the abused child or ghetto dweller has as much free will and ultimate responsibility for what he or she does as one who lives in more advantaged circumstances... The theory of this book implies no such consequence. Precisely because that theory recognises the embeddedness of free will in the natural order, it recognises that free will and moral responsibility are a matter of degree, and our possession of them can be very much influenced by circumstances. That is why, if one believes in the value of free will and ultimate responsibility, it is important to cultivate a social order in which they can flourish...

Kane (1998, page 213)

Chemical-Man

In Kane's libertarian theory, free will is a *contextual* property. This essential historical context, expressed in Kane's UR condition, is one way to distinguish a free choice from an act of chance.

By contextual, I mean that the fact that a person has free will depends not just on their ontological state (loosely, "complete experiential and physical state including brain state") at the present moment (which will determine their beliefs, thoughts, and even the probabilities that they will take particular actions in the given situation). Free will also crucially depends on the person having an authentic life-history, so that these beliefs are indeed based on prior free decisions. This is analogous to a painting that is an exact molecule for molecule replica of a painting by Picasso. The replica will rightly have less value because it does not have the correct provenance. The value of a painting is thus another example of a contextual property.

Here is a somewhat fantastical philosophical thought experiment. Suppose that a scientist were able to create a human adult, by mixing chemicals in a vat. This Chemical-Man would have memories, beliefs, values, and drives. However, he would have no responsibility for any of these things, because they result solely from the actions of the scientist. The memories for example, although experientially normal, would be entirely false.

Suppose that, soon after his creation, the Chemical-Man were to kill someone. I would argue that the Chemical-Man would be not be guilty of murder, even if he were molecule-for-molecule indistinguishable from a Natural-Man, whose memories, beliefs, values, drives, and even propensities to behave were identical. By supposition, the Natural-Man differs only in that he has had a normal history, so that his memories are veridical. In contrast to the Chemical-Man, the Natural-Man would be guilty of murder if he deliberately killed someone.

I believe that our commonsense human understanding enables us to recognize this contextual difference between Chemical-Man and Natural-Man. Both men have an equal understanding of the consequences of their actions. But Chemical-Man lacks free will because he has had no genuine prior interaction with the world. Free will would only develop gradually in Chemical-Man after he had spent a significant time interacting freely with others.

Our legal system also reflects this historical context, if somewhat crudely. Clearly our laws do not deal with Chemical-Man, but children are somewhat similar in that they have only limited free will (in the sense of UR) because they have only a limited history of interaction with the world. It is almost universally accepted that people are only regarded as being criminally responsible for their actions once they have reached a certain age. This is true in general despite the fact that the age of criminal responsibility varies considerably (between about 7 and 21 years) for different crimes and for different cultures.

To sum up, a molecule for molecule (or even quantum state for quantum state) replica of a given human being would have qualitatively identical beliefs, experiences, memories, drives, desires, and propensities to behave. It is even equally *free* in the sense of AP to act in one way or another in the current situation. The replica, however, would lack *free will* because it lacks UR: its propensities to behave have not arisen, as is the case for a normal human, out of a long history of free acts in the past.

(Chemical-Man is essentially the same as the famous Swamp-Man proposed by Donald Davidson in *Knowing One's Own Mind* (Lycan, 1999, page 385). Davidson's radical proposal is that consciousness itself is a contextual property, so that a perfect molecule-for-molecule replica of a human being, created by a freak accident in a swamp, would not even be conscious. I do not support this idea, which relies on a specific contextual definition of consciousness.)

Reconciliation of the FW and PS viewpoints

Now at last we are ready to complete the reconciliation of the two worldviews of a human person, both as an agent with libertarian free will (FW), and as a physical system (PS).

Reconciliation of these viewpoints can be separated into aspects that are listed below:

• **Free will is not independent of physics**

Some early philosophers wrongly suggest this independence. For example Descartes appealed to the human soul, interacting with the physical brain within the pineal gland, as being the source of free will. Stapp's model requires no such transcendental agency: see Stapp (2004a, page 21). Moreover, as we are interpreting it here, Stapp's theory is not independent of physics; see the remarks on lawlessness in the section **Physical systems** above.

Having free will independent of physics has undesirable ethical consequences. It means that everyone performing a specific wicked act is equally guilty no matter what mitigating circumstances there might be. There would be no concept of diminished responsibility in the cases of an appalling upbringing, a serious mental illness, or even of severe brain damage. Kane explicitly states that our freedom is conditional on our opportunities. For example, Kane's theory *predicts* that the objective physical situation of being brought up as a ghetto child will usually limit that child's free will.

- **The meanings of the words "random" and of "choice"**

Random in the context of physics means that there is a theoretical probability p that a certain event will occur. The experiment is performed N times, and the event happens in n of these experiments. As n increases, the ratio n/N approaches p. Moreover, there is no supplementary measurement that can be made to determine whether or not the event will occur in any particular experiment.

For example, a photon approaches a half-silvered mirror, and the event in question is that the photon will be reflected. For this event, the probability p = ½. There is no additional measurement that can be made to predict whether or not a particular photon will be reflected.

A *choice* is simply that – a choice based on sentience. According to idealist panpsychism the photon is an experiential entity making a free choice, based on its (extremely primitive) experience of the totality of its environment.

If no cause for an event can be determined within the discipline of physics, this does not imply that there is no cause at all. From the above definitions, there is nothing inconsistent in saying that an event that is random in the context of physics is in fact an authentic free choice based on sentience.

Someone who claims that randomness and choice are incompatible is usually (consciously or implicitly) defining random in the strong metaphysical sense that there is *no reason whatsoever* for the observed outcome. There is no evidence (scientific, philosophical or otherwise) for the truth of metaphysical randomness. Idealist panpsychists accept physical randomness but reject metaphysical randomness. This argument, already given in Chapter 8, applies as much to presidents as it does to particles.

- **The president's choice is made with mathematically definite probability p. Doesn't this detract from his freedom?**

The answer is *No* for two reasons. First, the president is in part responsible for creating his initial brain state P_1, and thus for the value of his personal probability p; see the discussion of **A human person** above. Second, it is not a matter of luck: he does not act by rolling a die or tossing a coin inside his head. The process he actually undertakes is of conscious thought, anguish, effort and moral responsibility. I agree with David Hodgson, who links quantum probabilities in like situations to the felt strength of reasons, (1991, page 393).

- **Free will is a contextual property, not just dependent on the current brain state**

This has been discussed in the **Chemical-Man** section. An adult person has free will by way of the specific history of free choices made throughout his or her lifetime. Kane calls each of these essential, historical choices a *self-forming action* **(SFA)**; see Kane (1998, pages 75-7).

Every self-forming action is recorded in memory, (Stapp, 2004a, page 129), and so the person has been a co-creator of all his memories, and thus of his current brain configuration. He is co-creator of his current stream of consciousness, and thus of his propensities to act in one way rather than another. (The term "co-creator" is used here because heredity and environment are also important factors in creating a person's current experiential state. In particular, a person might have diminished responsibility if his upbringing were impoverished.)

Free will (in the sense of UR) is absent in newborn babies, but emerges over the course of a loving childhood. Newborn babies have what Kane describes a "wanton" AP freedom without UR (1998, page 62). Free will is never perfect, but we are never too old to nurture and develop our freedom further. Thus we may strive towards wisdom.

11

Sensuous Cosmos

For in and out, above, about, below,
'Tis nothing but a Magic Shadow-show,
Play'd in a Box whose Candle is the Sun,
Round which we Phantom Figures come and go.

The Rubáiyát of Omár Khayyám

Our ship rests at anchor in the lee of an unknown isle, where we are refilling the hold with fresh water and food, and have an opportunity to rest and reflect on our journey. We can take delight in the honeyed taste of ripe mangoes before sailing on into uncharted waters. I have come to the limits of my present knowledge on this voyage of discovery from the material world towards the sensuous cosmos, but soon we must embark once more and continue our quest. What is the nature of our universe; and who are we, the creatures who dwell within it?

The materialist or physicalist metaphor is that the universe and everything within it, including ourselves, is a deterministic machine, trapped from the beginning to the end of time on the rigid tracks of inviolable laws. Only the mechanisms of physics – fields of force, electrical charges, and so on – are important; nothing else matters. Hopes, fears, choices, tastes, sights, touch, experiences of beauty and suffering: everything concerning the mind is an illusion, or is at best a useless and absurd epiphe-nomenon.

In the sensuous cosmos, the essence of our being is that we can experience the world in all its exquisite, sensual beauty and unbearable suffering – both natural and caused by human actions. It is a world in which we actively participate as rational agents with limited but authentic freedom. The future of our own small planet is not fully determined. Collectively we have it in our power to make it heaven or hell, as we wish. We are essentially a community of spiritual beings, interacting with one another and with other beings, all of them spiritual. We perceive each other as physical bodies, but when we interact with one another most intimately, both in speech and in touch, we know the literal truth that we are "such stuff as dreams are made on."

This chapter evaluates physicalism against idealist panpsychism, pointing out the substantial weaknesses of the former, and summarizing the arguments in favor of the latter. Doubts about the plausibility of idealist panpsychism and its consistency with current scientific knowledge are laid to rest. There are some suggestions for further reading on panpsychism, and a discussion of Berkeley's idealism. Some technical points, omitted from previous chapters, are then dealt with briefly. There is a section on idealist panpsychism and David Chalmers' "hard problem". Finally, I say some more about the spirit of the age, and close by briefly alluding to my own personal faith.

Physicalism

Physicalism is the thesis that the objects that exist within the universe are ultimately composed of insensate entities that are fully describable in terms of (completed) physics. Such insensate ultimates include particles such as quarks, or fields such as an electromagnetic field. Mind, when and where it exists, is fully determined by the spatiotemporal configuration of these insensate ultimates. Contrary to popular belief, physicalism is not part of science. Physicalism is a philosophical (specifically metaphysical) position. We can contrast physicalism with the alternative metaphysical position of idealist panpsychism by asking ourselves which of them gives the most plausible and comprehensive account, consistent with our current scientific knowledge, of those problems that call for an explanation. (Such problems include those of qualia, mental causation, existence, human freedom, and the mind-body problem. How these problems are expressed, and the manner of the attempt to resolve them, will both depend strongly on the metaphysical position taken.)

Physicalism tries to improve on Descartes' two-substance theory by eliminating mind-stuff, and by explaining mind in terms of matter (broadly construing "matter" as being any of the insensate ultimates of physics). For several hundred years (from 1687 to 1927), following the success of Isaac Newton's description of matter as "solid, massy, hard, impenetrable, moveable particles" – in other words characterizing atoms as analogous to billiard balls as naively experienced – it seemed as though physicalism was a success in accounting for and modeling the behavior of entities within the universe. In the twentieth century it became clear that this success could no longer hold. This was for two reasons.

First, with the advent of quantum theory, there is no longer an undisputed characterization of matter as it exists independently of human observers. We can now only say that, if we set up a particular experimental situation, then we will experience matter behaving in certain ways, according to propensities describable by certain equations. As discussed in Chapters 2 and 8, within quantum theory we have an accepted epistemology but no agreed ontology. Thus current-day science, surprisingly, gives physicalism no clear concept of matter with which to work. Without this, there is no clear concept of the existence of anything in the universe. What is water? Water is made up from molecules, which are made up from atoms, which are made up from elementary particles (or perhaps other ultimates, such as strings). But what are these ultimates in themselves, and not in relation to human observation? If we cannot answer this question then we do not know precisely what water is in itself. But surely water must be *something* in itself? After all, water was essential in order for us to have evolved, and so water must exist as something absolute and definite in the absence of humans.

Second, despite many efforts, particularly over the past three decades, physicalism has made no progress with what David Chalmers calls the "hard problem" of consciousness. Things are no better for physicalists since Thomas Huxley remarked in 1866 that, "How it is that anything so remarkable as a state of consciousness comes about as a result of irritating nervous tissue, is just as unaccountable as the appearance of the Djin when Aladdin rubbed his lamp," (Seager, 1999, page 256). Moreover, with no proper account of matter or of consciousness, physicalists cannot give an adequate account of mental causation. Some physicalists deny the reality of mental causation. There are also surprisingly many books on consciousness, written by authors who explicitly or implicitly take the physicalist position, that do not broach the topic of mental causation at all.

Idealist panpsychism

One way to approach idealist panpsychism is to say that it departs from Cartesian dualism by traveling in the opposite direction to physicalism. Instead of eliminating mind-stuff, idealist panpsychism eliminates matter-stuff! More precisely, the theory takes minds (centers of experience) as being funda-mental. It then re-characterizes "matter" as being nothing more than the empirical existence of minds to other minds. In particular, minds do not have to be "cloaked in matter" in order to be perceived by other minds: it is just a brute fact that minds cause percepts in other minds. There are no "substances" as such in the universe. Instead, every object within the cosmos is composed entirely of hierarchies of experiential entities (minds) of greater or lesser complexity. The simplest experiential entities correspond to the ultimate entities of physics.

Idealist panpsychism thus has a clear concept of the actual or concrete existence of things in the world. An object exists if and only if it is a (perhaps very primitive) experiential entity (or is composed of such entities). Everything with empirical existence, that is to say everything whose existence is inferred directly or indirectly from regularities in the experiences of human beings (examples include a hedgehog, a rock, a ruler, a water molecule, and an electron), is in fact either an experiential entity, or is composed of experiential entities.

This foundation removes the need to explain consciousness per se because it is fundamental to the universe. Instead this book has attempted to explain physics in terms of mind. We have defined consciousness broadly. Recall from Chapter 2 that any entity possessing any mental content whatsoever, perhaps possessing no more than some raw sensation, will be said to be *conscious* and to possess *mind*. Idealist panpsychism makes the assertion that, intrinsically, all objects are experiential entities analogous to us as experiential entities, but whose experiences and freedom to act are very much simpler. Human beings (as persons) and elementary particles thus belong to the same existential category.

Mental causation was discussed in Chapters 6 and 10. In idealist panpsychism all true causation is mental causation between interacting experiential entities, as was shown in Figure 6.4. Strict reductionism is true, but physics is only about the mathematical description of the appearances of things to human beings, and even completed physics can do no more than describe veridical appearances (the empirical phenomena). There is thus what I have called "rabbit-hole reductionism" where we must descend to the level beneath appearances to find the underlying reality. In our own case we know that we are experiential entities, and so we take it that all existence is of this same character. To exist is to be an experiential entity, experiencing and interacting with other experiential entities, and there is nothing else in the universe. So-called physical causation comprises lawful regularities among appearances that are explained by the underlying actual causation between experiential entities. Physical causation is thus analogous to the silhouette of a bat seeming to cause the silhouette of a ball to change direction.

Plausibility

Isn't idealist panpsychism implausible compared with physicalism, and isn't it incompatible with science?

I believe that any seeming implausibility of idealist panpsychism stems from three sources. First, we implicitly suppose that physics has, or eventually will have, an immediate and complete grasp of the objects that it discusses. Once we imagine that we know what an electron is, and that this knowledge does not involve any sentience, then the possibility that an electron might be sentient seems absurd. But, as I have repeatedly argued, physics is empirical and deals strictly with phenomena or appearances, and it does not provide us with any knowledge of what an electron actually is. The struggle during which physicists gave up the claim to be able to provide such ontological knowledge was hard fought among titans of physics Einstein and Bohr during the Solvay conference of 1927, and it is generally and reluctantly accepted that Niels Bohr won the argument. Despite Bohr's warnings there is still a tendency for some physicists to believe that science can or will of itself provide an ontology for the universe.

Second, we still tend to try to visualize what subatomic particles are like, and our limited imagination clings to Newton's picture of them as miniature billiard balls. We forget the uncanny ability of these particles both to "feel out" all possible routes through an elaborate experimental set-up, and to combine with other particles into entangled entities with a single, indecomposable state, as outlined in Chapter 8. These strange powers are not sufficient in themselves to prove panpsychism true, but they are mysterious in terms of physicalism and yet are to be expected with panpsychism. They therefore give evidential weight to panpsychism, if we already have other reasons to believe in the theory. Such prior reasons were given in Chapters 4 and 5.

Third, simply because of its familiarity, we ignore or forgive the vast implausibility and many weaknesses of physicalism as a philosophy. What do we mean by "matter" or "physical" or "existence"? Is there any physicalist account of consciousness that lays to rest Thomas Huxley's incredulity as to how it might arise from insensate matter? Physicalism is deeply rooted in our present culture, and even many scientists who should know better wrongly amalgamate physicalism with science. They assert that science has proven physicalism (sometimes called materialism) to be true. In doing so, they confuse scientific theories with metaphysical positions.

Is idealist panpsychism compatible with present day science? It is. Please refer to the **Philosophical viewpoints** section in Chapter 5, and in particular to the quotations from Arthur Eddington and David Chalmers. As the physicist Eddington emphasizes:

> There is nothing to prevent the assemblage of atoms constituting a brain from being of itself a thinking object in virtue of that nature which physics leaves undetermined and undeterminable.
>
> (1928, page 260).

A library of panpsychism

Panpsychism has always been a minority undercurrent of Western philosophy. Here is a brief reading list, describing some influential books.

David Skrbina (2005) has written a history of panpsychism in Western philosophy. He begins with the ancient Greeks, including Epicurus who wrote of atoms having the freedom to "swerve." Renaissance thinkers include Bruno, Spinoza and Leibniz. Panpsychism was very influential at the end of the nineteenth century, with proponents including Schopenhauer and William James. Skrbina makes clear that James' views in the latter part of his life (1901-1910) are close to the ideas developed here. James affirmed an increasingly-explicit panpsychic "radical empiricism" in which, "Individual minds and the hierarchy of lower- and higher-order mind constitute the reality of the cosmos" and "everything consists of pure experience," (Skrbina, 2005, pages 145-9). In the twentieth century, important figures include Alfred North Whitehead, Teilhard de Chardin and, most recently, Galen Strawson.

Alfred North Whitehead, most notably in *Process and Reality* (1929), develops a particular, complex theory of panpsychism into a system of metaphysics that is as complete as possible. Unfortunately, his writing is sometimes obscure because he invents many new words and uses them without giving examples. In *Unsnarling the World Knot* (1998), David Ray Griffin gives a clearer exposition of Whitehead's ideas, and includes some developments of his own. According to Whitehead and Griffin, the ultimate constituents of nature, called "occasions of experience", are mind-like in their essential character. They lack full consciousness, but can "experience" (Griffin) or "prehend" (Whitehead) their environment. Their existence is only momentary. They make choices in the light of their primitive experiences and are then extinguished to become part of the history of the universe as physical objects. Each discrete occasion (or moment) of experience thus has both a mental and a physical aspect (Whitehead calls these aspects "poles"): what is experiential in character at the present moment becomes physical when it has departed into the past, and becomes the basis for new occasions of experience. A long-lived particle such as an electron is in reality composed of a succession of occasions of experience of a particular type.

D.S. Clarke has written two accessible books on panpsychism. One of them, *Panpsychism – Past and Recent Selected Readings* (2004), is a history of panpsychism, given in terms of readings together with commentaries. His other book, *Panpsychism and the Religious Attitude* (2003), is as the title suggests. Christian de Quincey's *Radical Nature* (2002), which is the first book in a trilogy, is a non-technical argument in favor of panpsychism along the lines set out by Whitehead and Griffin. He also includes a history of the subject. The book is notable for the extensive discussion he gives to the relationship between panpsychism and idealism, particularly throughout his Chapter 9.

Thomas Nagel's book *Mortal Questions* (1979) contains a chapter on panpsychism. He gives a short, four-step argument for panpsychism, although, in the end, he decides that he could not come down unequivocally in the theory's favor. His argument has already been alluded to in Chapter 2. In his Gifford Lectures of 1927, published as *The Nature of the Physical World* (1928), Arthur Eddington supports panpsychism, and discusses numerous related ideas. In the book *Consciousness and Its Place in Nature* (2006), Galen Strawson strongly advocates panpsychism, arguing against the possibility that consciousness might have emerged, and he passionately criticizes physicalists such as Dennett for effectively denying that consciousness exists. In making his case, Strawson presents arguments similar to Nagel's, and quotes Eddington extensively. Strawson's book was originally published as a special double issue of the *Journal of Consciousness Studies* (Vol. 13 No. 10-11).

Explaining Consciousness – the "Hard Problem", edited by Jonathan Shear (1997) contains David Chalmers' seminal paper, together with responses to it. Surprisingly many of these responses refer to panpsychism. In his later paper *An Argument for Idealism* (2001), John Bolender presents some ideas very close to those expressed here.

A fairly representative set of books on panpsychism can be fitted onto a one-foot bookshelf. For a wider selection see the references here (or those given by Skrbina, 2005).

Berkeley's idealism

In 1710 Bishop George Berkeley first published his *Principles of Human Knowledge*, defending *idealism*, the position that everything is composed of mind (or soul). In addition to human minds there is also, importantly, the mind of God. Berkeley argued that it was meaningless to assert that something exists when it is not being observed. Objects of physical experience (examples include a mouse, a rock, a ruler, and water) exist as ideas or percepts in the minds of humans. What sort of existence do these objects have when they are not being observed by us? Berkeley argued that they existed solely as ideas in the mind of God.

In this way, thanks to the grace of God, a ruler locked in a desk drawer would again be perceived when the drawer is reopened. Berkeley did not believe in the existence of anything that could not be directly observed. For him, had he known about them, such things as molecules and electrons would be mere abstractions.

Berkeley was scathing about the vagueness of what physicalist philosophers meant by the words "matter" and "substance". Moreover God would not need any material water (whatever that might be) in order to understand the developing physical state of an unobserved ocean, any more than a mathematician would need to use her fingers in order to multiply two by three.

We can contrast Berkeley's idealism with idealist panpsychism:

- Berkeley claims that it is meaningless to talk about entities when they are not being observed. According to idealist panpsychism, some meaning can be given, but unobserved existence amounts to no more than a mathematical abstraction (see Chapter 4).

- Berkeley's idealism is inhomogeneous in that two types of things exist: (1) Minds or souls of humans and of God; (2) Objects such as rocks that exist solely as regularities in the percepts or ideas within minds. For such object, "to be is to be perceived." Idealist panpsychism is homogeneous: Everything that exists is a mind that has structured percepts and can be perceived by other minds. Rocks and human beings differ only in their complexity, and not in their fundamental category of existence. As a universal rule "To exist is to perceive and to be perceived."

- In Berkeley's idealism, there is an essential overarching cosmic mind, called *God*. For Berkeley himself, God has all the attributes of Christian theology, such as omnipotence and beneficence. Idealist panpsychism makes no reference to a cosmic mind, (although I myself have a religious faith).

For Berkeley, chemicals such as carbon and water are purely ideas in the minds of humans and of God: they have no independent existence and are not in themselves minds. Berkeley would therefore find it impossible to explain human evolution or development without requiring a special intervention by God in order to give an independently existing mind to each person. According to Berkeley, a baby or fetus, before it is given a soul by God's intervention, is no more than a collection of ideas in other minds. God's intervention adds a mind [which is of Berkeley's existential type (1)] to an object [which is of Berkeley's existential type (2)].

With idealist panpsychism the evolution of human consciousness is no more than the evolution of complex experiential entities from very simple experiential entities. The possibility of giving a naturalistic account of the evolution of mind from basic chemicals is a major advantage of idealist panpsychism over Berkeley's idealism. The same argument applies to the development of an adult human from a single cell.

Idealism was a popular philosophical position in the late nineteenth century, but since then it has gone decidedly out of fashion. In the twentieth century, the most famous exponent of idealism was A.J. Ayer. Nowadays, idealism is frequently dismissed in a sentence or two as a ridiculous philosophy. In such dismissals, idealism is often identified with Berkeley's idealism, but there are many other variations of idealism using very different concepts. In particular, idealist panpsychism does not deny the reality of rocks. Indeed, by comparison with physicalism, idealist panpsychism gives a much more lucid explanation of what is meant by the claim that a rock is real (see Chapter 4).

Some technical points

We can now clear up a few remaining technical points about idealist panpsychism and about consciousness in general that have not been fully explained earlier.

The first topic is *supervenience*. David Chalmers states that:

> In general, supervenience is a relation between two sets of properties: B-properties – intuitively high-level properties – and A-properties, which are the more basic low-level properties...
>
> B-properties supervene on A-properties if no two possible situations are identical with respect to their A-properties while differing in their B-properties.

David Chalmers (1996, page 33)

In most theories of consciousness, mind arises from and is thus determined by the physical state of the brain. The dependency does not go in the other direction. Two distinct brain states can give rise to the same state of mind, and thus mental state does not determine brain state. For these essentially physicalist theories mental states supervene on brain states.

In contrast, with idealist panpsychism, physical states, including brain states, arise as the appearances to other human beings of the hierarchies of experiential entities that constitute the essence of a human brain. Because two different realities can have the same appearance for human observers, it follows that physical brain states supervene on the (totality of the) mental states that constitute the essence of that brain. It follows that, no matter how thorough, a detailed physical examination of a human brain is never enough to determine uniquely its under-lying mental states. This is inconvenient for scientists, but it fits in with Heisenberg's quantum indeterminacy principle that the physical examination of any system can never be complete and perfect.

Another contentious theoretical issue in the philosophy of consciousness is the possible existence of *philosophical zombies*. These are putative creatures who behave in exactly the same manner as human beings, but who have no inner mental life. They can weep and talk seemingly passionately about pain, or rhapsodize about the exquisite taste of lamb chops, or write treatises about consciousness, and yet they have no minds. There is nothing like there is to be a zombie, not even an existential void. Theories that admit the possibility of zombies are in deep trouble, because this indicates that consciousness, where it exists, must be a useless epiphenomenon.

The physicalist Dennett's *Consciousness Explained* (1991) takes an ambiguous attitude towards zombies. At one point he asserts, "We are all zombies," (page 406) but more often he denies that zombies are possible. Dennett redefines consciousness in strictly behaviorist terms. According to him zombies are ridiculous because there is no conceptual difference between a zombie and a non-zombie. I find Dennett's position strange because logically he should say it is non-zombies that are ridiculous.

According to idealist panpsychism, zombies are impossible because by definition to *exist* in any universe is to be an experiential entity, no more no less. Take away mind from any entity, and you have removed the entity itself.

Some physicalists including Patricia Churchland have argued that a *lack of imagination* about the possible future scope of science prevents many philosophers from seeing that there might in the future be a reductionist and physicalist account of consciousness that includes a satisfactory explanation of qualia. The answer is that reduction to the level of physics amounts to expressing our common experiences of the world in terms of mathematical equations. We can imagine very well in general terms what future mathematical equations might be like. They might become more elegant and complex, but mathematical equations will never become a tickle or a pain. In the same way, we know in general terms what can be made out of Lego bricks. Doubtless some wondrous structures can be made, intricate beyond our current powers of imagination. But we do already know that no one in the distant future, no matter how intelligent, will ever be able to make a banana milkshake from Lego bricks.

Related to the above, some people argue that *psychology* might provide a scientific solution to the problem of consciousness. However, if you examine its foundations, you will see that psychology does not attempt to reduce or explain consciousness. Rather it takes consciousness as given, and as revealed by a critical-realist interpretation of the speech and behavior of its subjects. Psychology is essential to understanding the structure of our consciousness, particularly the significant ways in which we can be greatly deluded about it, but psychology makes no attempt to explain it. For example, in his groundbreaking work *The Principles of Psychology* William James writes (emphasis original):

> *Every natural science assumes certain data uncritically, and declines to challenge the elements between which its own "laws" obtain, and from which its own deductions are carried on. Psychology, the science of finite individual minds, assumes as its data (1)* thoughts and feelings, *and (2)* a physical world in time and space with which they coexist and which (3) *they* know. *Of course, these data themselves are discussable; but the discussion of them is called metaphysics and falls outside the province of this book.*
>
> William James (1983 [1890], page 6)

The hard problem revisited

Recall from Chapter 2 that David Chalmers points out that much scientific progress does not touch the essence of consciousness:

> *Many books and articles on consciousness have appeared in the past few years and one might think that we are making progress. But on a closer look, most of this work leaves the hardest problems about consciousness untouched. Often the work addresses what might be called the "easy" problems of consciousness: How does the brain process environmental stimulations? How does it integrate information? How do we produce reports on internal states? These are important questions, but to answer them is not to solve the hard problem: Why is all this processing accompanied by an experienced inner life?*
>
> David Chalmers (1996, pages xi – xii)

Most forms of panpsychism fall into the same trap. Mind is proposed as an extra feature or property possessed by the ultimate elementary entities of physics. Scientists will object that no such extra ingredient has been detected. Moreover, they can explain the behavior of physical ultimates without recourse to this extra ingredient. The sentience of ultimates must therefore be epiphenomenal, and this position has been decisively rejected in Chapter 6. With most forms of panpsychism, Chalmers' objection still holds.

Idealist panpsychism takes a more radical, specifically metaphysical approach. Instead of being an extra feature, on a par with mass or charge, mind (broadly conceived) constitutes the essence of what a physical ultimate actually is. Take away an electron's mind, therefore, and you have taken away the electron itself. Without a (very simple) experienced inner life, there would be no electron, and therefore no electron behavior, and therefore no physics for this electron.

In order to solve the mind-body problem, David Chalmers' question, "Why is all this processing accompanied by an experienced inner life?" needs to be reversed. Instead, we need to ask ourselves, "How can interacting minds give rise to a system of physics, and in particular to the physical processes that are going on inside a human brain?"

The answer to this latter question is, was given in Chapter 6. It may be summarized:

> The universe is composed entirely of entities whose essence is that they have percepts. Whenever these entities interact or combine with one another, these changes in their configuration cause corresponding changes in the appearances that they present to other minds. These changing appearances constitute the empirical existence of these processes. For panpsychists, empirical existence amounts to physical existence because there is no corner of the universe where entities do not empirically exist. Eventually scientists evolve who are sophisticated enough to communicate with one another and to propose laws to explain their shared experiences. A system of physics for the universe,

which was latent from the beginning of time, thus becomes
evident. The physical/empirical processes that become manifest
include processes within the brains of humans.

This summary reminds me of Bertrand Russell who, late in his
life and somewhat atypically, wrote that, "The brain consists of
thoughts," (Ayer, 1972, page 114). Idealist panpsychists would
extend Russell's claim and assert that, "Everything consists of
thoughts."

Sailing on into uncharted waters

How can we make further progress with idealist panpsychism? I
can only make some tentative suggestions:

If panpsychism is true, then in studying physics at even the
most fundamental level we are studying simple forms of experiential entities. Each such entity would have a private, structured,
informationally incomplete, perspectival (or subjective), qualitative percept of its environment, and would make primitive
choices in the light of this percept. (A naïve, highly simplified
example of such a percept was given in the dodecahedral
example of Chapter 5.) We could guess at and make mathematical models of such percepts. We would never be able to
make any measurements to confirm directly such percepts, but
perhaps we could still develop a theory that would satisfy us
because of its consistency with experiment.

Primitive consciousness would be relevant to the behavior of
everything from molecules to viruses to single-celled organisms,
and we would particularly expect it to be revealed in their
holistic behavior.

There is also the difficult problem of discovering laws
explaining how perceptual structures of experiential ultimates
can be combined to give rise to the percepts of more complex
entities, and eventually to the consciousness of a human being.
Throughout the entire body of a human being there will be many

centers of perceptual experience arranged in hierarchies, with the most sophisticated being located within the brain. At the apex of these latter, there will be one or more probably several centers that generate the reportable human stream of consciousness.

The mathematical structure of the consciousness of elementary entities, and the laws by which these structures combine, might conceivably be guessed at. Going on to argue plausibly that these guessed laws are correct will be fiendishly difficult, but not "hard" in the sense of David Chalmers. For David Chalmers a "hard problem" is one that we do not have a scintilla of an idea how to approach. I have only touched upon the combination problem in this book, but quantum approaches such as Stapp's seem to hold promise.

The spirit of the age

The dominant spirit and philosophy of our age is physicalist in character. Proponents such as Daniel Dennett, Richard Dawkins and Peter Atkins rightly proclaim the successes of science, but wrongly identify science with the philosophical standpoints of both physicalism and secularism. They go on to make the tendentious assertion that science is the only possible source of knowledge, and that everything else, from religious faith to the arts and humanities, is empty of any meaning. Atkins, after affirming that science works by the slow accumulated progress of experiment and verification, says that:

> *Whether scientists will ever comprehend our joy of compre-hending the world, of acting out our lives within it, and all the other great questions that philosophers, artists, prophets, and theologians consider to be their territory of discourse is a matter for idle speculation. And we all know how useful that has been.*
>
> Peter Atkins (2003, page 2)

In writing this book, I wish to provide a counterweight to this physicalist tendency, and to propose a rational account of ourselves as spiritual beings, able to a limited extent to make genuine choices that give shape, meaning, value and direction to the courses of our lives. We are not helpless passengers whose lives are determined absolutely and entirely by our genes and our environment. Former Archbishop of York John Habgood sums up this position:

> *Our total genetic identity may endow us with some of our physical characteristics, and with some traits and dispositions rather than others, but what we actually become depends on what happens to us, what we do, the culture and physical environment in which we develop, and the personal relationships within which we stand.*
>
> John Habgood in David Lorimer, Ed. (2004, page 241)

Here I am assuming that "what we do" is John Habgood's brief affirmation of our human freedom to choose, both ethically and intellectually, and that "the culture and physical environment in which we develop," along with the other things he mentions, illustrate how these choices may be limited, particularly if our development is impoverished.

The difference between the physicalist and spiritual views of human nature is not just a theoretical matter. The way in which people perceive themselves can influence the way they speak about themselves and behave. An interviewee on the UK's Radio Four recently calmly asserted, "I found myself doing armed robberies." But armed robbery requires conscious, rational planning, and is not the kind of thing one can just find oneself doing, as one might find oneself humming a tune. The philosophy of physicalism is not responsible for this man's behavior – he is. Yet the physicalist ambience in which we presently live makes it plausible for him to claim this passive moral helplessness. In his book *Mindful Universe*, Henry Stapp says:

> *More than three quarters of a century have passed since the overturning of mechanical laws, yet the notion of mechanical determinism still dominates the general intellectual milieu. The inertia of that superseded physical theory continues to affect your life in important ways. It still drives the decisions of governments, schools, courts, and medical institutions, and even your own choices, to the extent that you are influenced by what you are told by pundits who expound as scientific truth a mechanical idea of the universe that contravenes the precepts of contemporary physics.*
>
> Henry Stapp (2007, preface)

Human free will is not only important for the possibility of making moral choices, (which some philosophers deny). It is also crucial for human intellectual freedom. Why should anyone give credence to a verbally expressed proposition, if this is ultimately caused by mathematically controlled motions of molecules in a human brain? If physicalism is true, then surely the cause of any verbal assertion is the deterministic workings of physics, unrelated to the truth of that assertion. Moreover, if my verbal affirmation is entirely due the motion of matter in my brain, then in what sense can it *be a belief*, and in what sense can I *possess* or be responsible for it? How can I have the intellectual freedom to *evaluate and judge* what propositions to believe in? And what within physicalism might constitute such an evaluation and judgment?

Credo: a personal statement

Idealist panpsychism is a philosophical position, and is not tied to any particular faith, whether religious or secular. In this final section I will sketch my own provisional faith, after first giving some principles concerning the relationship between science, philosophy and faith.

Although these three subjects are interrelated, I believe that we should investigate them as far as possible in the order of their degree of certainty, that is to say, first the best of current-day science, next the best of philosophy illuminated by that science, and finally the best of faith that can be illuminated by both. Faith is an all-encompassing world-view and should be illuminated by all human endeavors, including the arts and humanities. When we speak within science, our words are supposed to have a specific meaning. In philosophy there is typically discussion as to what words mean. When we come to faith, words can no longer have a literal or exact meaning, and we must speak in terms of metaphor or poetry. This does not mean that our words mean nothing at all.

Science and its influence on philosophy have already been discussed. In his day Newton showed that the universe could be modeled by universal mathematical equations or laws that functioned independently of human observers. In the nineteenth and twentieth centuries respectively, Darwin and Einstein showed that both the universe and life within it are evolving. One can be either optimistic or pessimistic about this evolution: certainly the envelope of complexity and variety of life has tended to increase albeit with a few major setbacks, but it is almost certain that all life on this planet will be erased with the death of our Sun. There is only a small chance that a few of our descendents will escape to spread life throughout the universe, but the most probable eventual state of the universe will be as a dead husk.

Science at various points of history was thought to be more-or-less complete. In 1900 Lord Kelvin notoriously asserted that science was no longer interesting because every significant discovery had already been made, and only minor tidying-up remained to be done. Nowadays no one would assert such a thing. We do not even know the dimensionality of space, nor whether or not our own observable universe is a mere bubble in a much larger family of universes, each with its own related laws.

I believe that we need to recognize the necessity of faith. This necessity is a consequence of the inevitably limited and incomplete knowledge of the world provided by science and philosophy. During the course of our lives we nonetheless find ourselves needing to make choices and judgments that result in our performing specific acts. Only a faith on some sort can provide a principled motivation for such actions.

Faith is not just an intellectual pursuit. It is a lived experience among a community of those with similar views. We must also recognize the degree to which we nowadays live together in a close association with others from different faith traditions, both in our own neighborhood, and as part of the global community. I trust that there is sufficient truth in the different faith traditions for them to be useful guides for those who follow them, provided they take care not to let go of their critical faculties, and sift out the best of their tradition from the chaff. This includes the substantial number of people who follow a tradition that is entirely secular. Some academics, such as John Hick (1989) and Harold Coward (2000) have the ability to combine understanding from several traditions. For myself, however, I do not have the intellect or inclination to stray far from the religious Western tradition, besides, the remainder of my life is too short. I do not know enough about Buddhism or other non-theistic faiths to be able to recognize the good from the bad.

For theists, there is a razor's edge between trusting provisionally in the absolute goodness of God and the consequent necessity of following God's will, and in complete humility in realizing that we might be totally mistaken in our understanding of God's will. This does not mean we should neglect our own reason. The metaphor of God as a loving parent is

excellent. Children begin by loving their parents uncondi-
tionally; as they grow into adolescence they can form an increas-
ingly balanced judgment as to whether their parents are good or
bad. If upon reflection our lived experience of God were to be
that of a sadistic, hate-filled authority figure, then God would
become someone humanity would ultimately have to take a
stand against. Almost all reflective theists do not find this evil
image to be our experience, and so we continue in our faith.
(Sadly this argument is undermined by the considerable number
of benighted theists whose words and actions reveal little but
pride, hatred and cruelty, even as they claim to be following the
God of mercy and love.)

In the course of thinking about consciousness my opinions
have changed and continue to change. No one starts out
nowadays by being a panpsychist, still less an idealist. My views
on mental causation are of quite recent origin. My religious
beliefs have changed also, and from a secular humanist I have
become a Quaker. Speaking for myself alone, and for the present
moment, I do not believe in an afterlife, or that God intervenes
in the universe by directly changing the course of events.
Nonetheless, I am more than a Deist, as I believe in the efficacy
of prayer in aligning ourselves to the will of God, allowing us
better to become agents for good within the world community.
Quakers are unique in that we do not have our own sacred text,
but publish an anthology of thought, both historical and
modern, that is agreed upon and revised for each generation. In
this way, each generation can be involved in developing their
concept of faith, without being too quickly tempted by intellectual fashion. My faith can be summed up simply:

*Take heed, dear Friends, to the promptings of love and truth in
your hearts. Trust them as the leadings of God, whose Light
shows us our darkness and brings us to new life.*

ADVICE 1, Quakers, *Advices and Queries* (1995)

References

If a URL is given in addition to the reference, then page numbers given in the text refer to the document as it appears on the internet.

Atkins, P. (2003), *Galileo's Finger – The Ten Great Ideas of Science* (Oxford: Oxford University Press)

Audi, R. (Ed.) (1999, 2nd edition), *The Cambridge Dictionary of Philosophy* (Cambridge: Cambridge University Press)

Ayer, A. (1972), *Russell* (London: Fontana)

Baggott, J. (1992), *The Meaning of Quantum Theory* (Oxford: Oxford University Press)

Baldwin, T. (2004), *Stanford Encyclopedia of Philosophy: Moore* http://plato.stanford.edu/entries/moore#6

Bell, M., Gottfried, K. & Veltman, M. (Eds.) (2001), *John S. Bell on the Foundations of Quantum Mechanics* (London: World Scientific)

Berkeley, G. (1710/1996), *Principles of Human Knowledge* and *Three Dialogues* (Oxford: Oxford University Press)

Block, N., Flanagan, O. & Güzeldere, G. (Eds.) (1997), *The Nature of Consciousness – Philosophical Debates* (Cambridge MA: MIT Press)

Bohm, D. (1951/1989), *Quantum Theory* (New York: Dover)

Bohm, D. (1980), *Wholeness and the Implicate Order* (London: Routledge)

Bohm, D. & Hiley, B. (1993), *The Undivided Universe: An Ontological Interpretation of Quantum Theory* (London: Routledge)

Bolender, J. (2001), 'An Argument for Idealism', *Journal of Consciousness Studies*, **8** (4), pp. 37-61

Bouwmeester, D., Ekert, A. & Zeilinger, A. (Eds.) (2000), *The Physics of Quantum Information* (Berlin: Springer)

Chalmers, D. (1995), 'Facing Up to the Problem of Consciousness', *Journal of Consciousness Studies*, **2** (3), pp. 200-219

Chalmers, D. (1996), *The Conscious Mind – In Search of a Fundamental Theory* (Oxford: Oxford University Press)

Chalmers, D. (1997), 'Moving Forward on the Problem of Consciousness', *Journal of Consciousness Studies*, **4** (1), pp. 3-46

Churchland, P. (1996), 'The Hornswoggle Problem', *Journal of Consciousness Studies*, **3** (5-6), pp. 402-408

Clarke, D. (2003), *Panpsychism and the Religious Attitude* (New York: SUNY Press)

Clarke, D. (2004), *Panpsychism – Past and Recent Selected Readings* (New York: SUNY Press)

Clayton, P. (2004), *Mind and Emergence – From Quantum to Consciousness* (Oxford: Oxford University Press)

Cottingham, J. et al. (Eds.) (1991), *The Philosophical Writings of Descartes – Volume III, The Correspondence* (Cambridge: Cambridge University Press)

Coward, H. (2000), *Pluralism in the World Religions – A Short Introduction* (Oxford: Oneworld)

Crick, F. (1994), *The Astonishing Hypothesis – The Scientific Search for the Soul* (London: Simon & Schuster)

Crick, F. & Koch, C. (1990), 'Towards a Neurobiological Theory of Consciousness', *Seminars in the Neurosciences*, **2**, pp. 263-275

Crick, F. & Koch, C. (1992), 'The Problem of Consciousness', *Scientific American*, September 1992, pp. 110-117

Davies, P. & Brown, J. (Eds.) (1986), *The Ghost in the Atom* (Cambridge: Cambridge University Press)

Dennett, D. (1991), *Consciousness Explained* (Boston: Little Brown)

Dennett, D. (1992), 'The Unimagined Preposterousness of Zombies', *Journal of Consciousness Studies*, **2** (4), pp. 322-333

de Quincey, C. (2002), *Radical Nature – Rediscovering the Soul of Matter* (Vermont: Invisible Cities Press)

Eddington, A. (1928), *The Nature of the Physical World* (Cambridge: Cambridge University Press)

Everett, H. (1957), ''Relative State' Formulation of Quantum Mechanics', *Reviews of Modern Physics*, **29**, pp. 454-462

Feynman, R. (1990), *QED: The Strange Theory of Light and Matter* (London: Penguin)

Goodman, N. (1978), *Ways of Worldmaking* (Indianapolis: Hackett)

Gingerich, O. (2006), *God's Universe* (Cambridge MA: Harvard University Press)

Gregory, R. (Ed.) (1987), *The Oxford Companion to the Mind* (Oxford: Oxford University Press)

Griffin, D. (1998), *Unsnarling the World-Knot – Consciousness, Freedom and the Mind-Body Problem* (Berkeley CA: University of California Press)

Grush, R. & Churchland, P. (1995), 'Gaps in Penrose's Toiling', *Journal of Consciousness Studies*, **2** (1), pp. 10-29

Hawking, S. (1988), *A Brief History of Time: From the Big Bang to Black Holes* (London: Bantam)

Hawking, S. (2001), *The Universe in a Nutshell* (London: Bantam)

Hawking, S. & Ellis, G. (1973), *The Large Scale Structure of Space-Time* (Cambridge: Cambridge University Press)

Hick, J. (1989), *An Interpretation of Religion – Human Responses to the Transcendent* (London: MacMillan)

Hodgson, D. (1991), *The Mind Matters – Consciousness and Choice in a Quantum World* (Oxford: Oxford University Press)

Hodgson, D. (1996), 'The Easy Problems Ain't so Easy', *Journal of Consciousness Studies*, **3** (1), pp. 69-75

Hogben, L. (1936), *Mathematics for the Million* (London: George Allen & Unwin)

Horgan, J. (1999), *The Undiscovered Mind – How the Human Brain Defies Replication, Medication, and Explanation* (New York: Free Press)

Hut, P., Alford, M. & Tegmark, M. (2006), 'On Math, Matter and Mind', *Foundations of Physics*, **36**, pp. 765-794. http://arxiv.org/pdf/physics/0510188

James, W. (1890/1983), *The Principles of Psychology* (Cambridge MA: Harvard University Press)

Kane, R. (1998), *The Significance of Free Will* (Oxford: Oxford University Press)

Kane, R. (Ed.) (2002), *Free Will* (Oxford: Blackwell)

Kant, I. (A1781/B1787/1998), *Critique of Pure Reason* (Cambridge: Cambridge University Press)

Kim, J. (1996), *Philosophy of Mind* (Oxford: Westview Press)

Koch, C. (2004), 'Thinking About the Conscious Mind' (Review of Searle, 2004), *Science*, **306**, pp. 979-980

Leibniz, G. (1714), *Monadology*. English translation taken from http://www.marxists.org/reference/subject/philosophy/works/ge/leibniz.htm

Lorimer, D. (Ed.) (2004), *Science, Consciousness and Ultimate Reality* (Exeter: Imprint Academic)

Lycan, W. (Ed.) (1999, 2nd edition), *Mind and Cognition – An Anthology* (Oxford: Blackwell)

Mattuck, R. (1992), *A Guide to Feynman Diagrams in the Many-Body Problem* (New York: Dover)

McLaughlin, B. & Bartlett, G. (2004), 'Have Noë and Thompson Cast Doubts on the Neural Correlates of Consciousness Programme?', *Journal of Consciousness Studies*, **11** (1), pp. 56-67

Misner, C., Thorne, K. & Wheeler, J. (1973), *Gravitation* (San Francisco: Freeman)

Nagel, T. (1979), *Mortal Questions* (Cambridge: Cambridge University Press)

Noë, A. & Thompson, E. (2004), 'Are There Neural Correlates of Consciousness?', *Journal of Consciousness Studies*, **11** (1), pp. 3-28

Papineau, D. & Selina H. (2000), *Introducing Consciousness* (Cambridge: Icon Books)

Penrose, R. (1989), *The Emperor's New Mind: Concerning Computers, Minds and the Laws of Physics* (Oxford: Oxford University Press)

Penrose, R. (1995), *Shadows of the Mind – A Search for the Missing Science of Consciousness* (London: Vintage)

Penrose, R. (2004), *The Road to Reality – A Complete Guide to the Laws of the Universe* (London: Jonathan Cape)

Poland, J. (1994), *Physicalism: The Philosophical Foundations* (Oxford: Clarendon Press)

[Quakers] (1995), *Advices and Queries* (London: British Quakers)

[Quakers] (1999, 2nd edition), *Quaker Faith and Practice – the book of Christian Discipline of the Yearly Meeting of the Religious Society of Friends (Quakers) in Britain* (London: British Quakers)

Robinson, D. (2008), *Consciousness and Mental Life* (New York: Columbia University Press)

Rosenberg, G. (2004), *A Place for Consciousness – Probing the Deep Structure of the Natural World* (Oxford: Oxford University Press)

Russell, B. (1927/2007), *The Analysis of Matter* (Nottingham: Russell Press)

Savile, A. (2005), *Kant's Critique of Pure Reason – an Orientation to a Central Theme* (Oxford: Blackwell)

Seager, W. (1995), 'Consciousness, Information and Panpsychism', *Journal of Consciousness Studies*, **2** (3), pp. 272-88

Seager, W. (1999), *Theories of Consciousness – An Introduction and Assessment* (London: Routledge)

Seager, W. (2005), *Stanford Encyclopedia of Philosophy: Panpsychism*
http://plato.stanford.edu/entries/panpsychism

Searle, J. (1984), *Minds, Brains and Science* (Cambridge MA: Harvard University Press)

Searle, J. (1992), *The Rediscovery of the Mind* (Cambridge MS: MIT Press)

Searle, J. (1997), *The Mystery of Consciousness* (London: Granta Books)

Searle, J. (2002), 'Why I am Not a Property Dualist', *Journal of Consciousness Studies*, **9** (12), pp. 57-64

Searle, J. (2004), *Mind – A Brief Introduction* (Oxford: Oxford University Press)

Shear, J. (Ed.) (1997), *Explaining Consciousness – the "Hard Problem"* (Cambridge MA: MIT Press)

Skrbina, D. (2003), 'Panpsychism as an underlying theme in Western Philosophy – a survey paper' *Journal of Consciousness Studies*, **10** (3), pp. 4-46

Skrbina, D. (2005), *Panpsychism in the West* (Cambridge, MA: MIT Press)

Sprigge, T. (1983), *The Vindication of Absolute Idealism* (Edinburgh: Edinburgh University Press)

Stapp, H. (1993, 1st edition), *Mind, Matter and Quantum Mechanics* (Berlin: Springer)

Stapp, H. (1996), 'The Hard Problem: A Quantum Approach', *Journal of Consciousness Studies*, **3** (3), pp. 194-210

Stapp, H. (2004a, 2nd edition), *Mind, Matter and Quantum Mechanics* (Berlin: Springer)

Stapp, H. (2004b), 'Quantum Leaps in Philosophy of Mind – reply to Bourget's critique', *Journal of Consciousness Studies*, **11** (12), pp. 43-49

Stapp, H. (2007), *Mindful Universe – Quantum Mechanics and the Participating Observer* (Berlin: Springer)

Stoljar, D. (2001), *Stanford Encyclopedia of Philosophy: Physicalism* http://plato.stanford.edu/entries/physicalism

Stone, M. & Wolff, J. (Eds.) (2000), *The Proper Ambition of Science* (London: Routledge)

Strawson, G. (1994), *Mental Reality* (Cambridge MA: MIT Press)

Strawson, G. (2006), 'Realistic Monism: why Physicalism Entails Panpsychism', *Journal of Consciousness Studies*, **13** (10-11), pp. 3-31

Strawson, G. (2006), *Consciousness and Its Place in Nature* (Exeter: Imprint Academic)

Tegmark, M. (2003), 'Parallel Universes' in Barrow, J., Davies, P. & Harper, C. (Eds.) *Science and Ultimate Reality: From Quantum to Cosmos*, honoring John Wheeler's 90th birthday (Cambridge: Cambridge University Press) http://space.mit.edu/home/tegmark/multiverse.pdf

Vimal, R. (2009), 'Meanings Attributed to the Term 'Consciousness'', *Journal of Consciousness Studies*, **16** (5), pp. 9-27

Von Neumann, J. (1971), *Mathematical Foundations of Quantum Mechanics* (New Jersey: Princeton University Press)

Walter, S. & Heckmann, H. (Eds.) (2003), *Physicalism and Mental Causation – The Metaphysics of Mind and Action* (Exeter: Imprint Academic)

Weston, S. (1989), *Walking Tall – An Autobiography* (London: Bloomsbury)

Whitaker, A. (1996), *Einstein, Bohr and the Quantum Dilemma* (Cambridge: Cambridge University Press)

Whitehead, A. (1929/1978), *Process and Reality: An Essay in Cosmology – corrected edition* (New York: Free Press)

BOOKS

O is a symbol of the world, of oneness and unity. In different cultures it also means the "eye," symbolizing knowledge and insight. We aim to publish books that are accessible, constructive and that challenge accepted opinion, both that of academia and the "moral majority."

Our books are available in all good English language bookstores worldwide. If you don't see the book on the shelves ask the bookstore to order it for you, quoting the ISBN number and title. Alternatively you can order online (all major online retail sites carry our titles) or contact the distributor in the relevant country, listed on the copyright page.

See our website www.o-books.net for a full list of over 500 titles, growing by 100 a year.

And tune in to myspiritradio.com for our book review radio show, hosted by June-Elleni Laine, where you can listen to the authors discussing their books.